MODERN CLASSIC SONATAS

BOOK 4

Dr. Anis I. Milad

authorHOUSE®

AuthorHouse™
1663 Liberty Drive
Bloomington, IN 47403
www.authorhouse.com
Phone: 1 (800) 839-8640

"This book "Modern Classic Sonatas - Book 3 and Book 4" includes sonatas which were composed by Dr. Anis I. Milad. Dr. Milad expressed his emotion and was able to complete each sonata in three parts "exposition, development, and recapitulation" and in a variety of Key Signature. These sonatas are also published in YouTube. Producing books to include this form of music is a door for the new generations to follow and improve the classic music. This book is also produced to get the attention of the conductors and the musicians around the world to our world in the United States of America"

Published by AuthorHouse 07/12/2019

ISBN: 978-1-7283-1878-3 (sc)
ISBN: 978-1-7283-1877-6 (e)

Print information available on the last page.

Contents

Score

Sonata No 35, Op 282 - I Am Not Angry - Part 1

Dr. Anis I. Milad

11
D.B.
Picc.
S
14
17

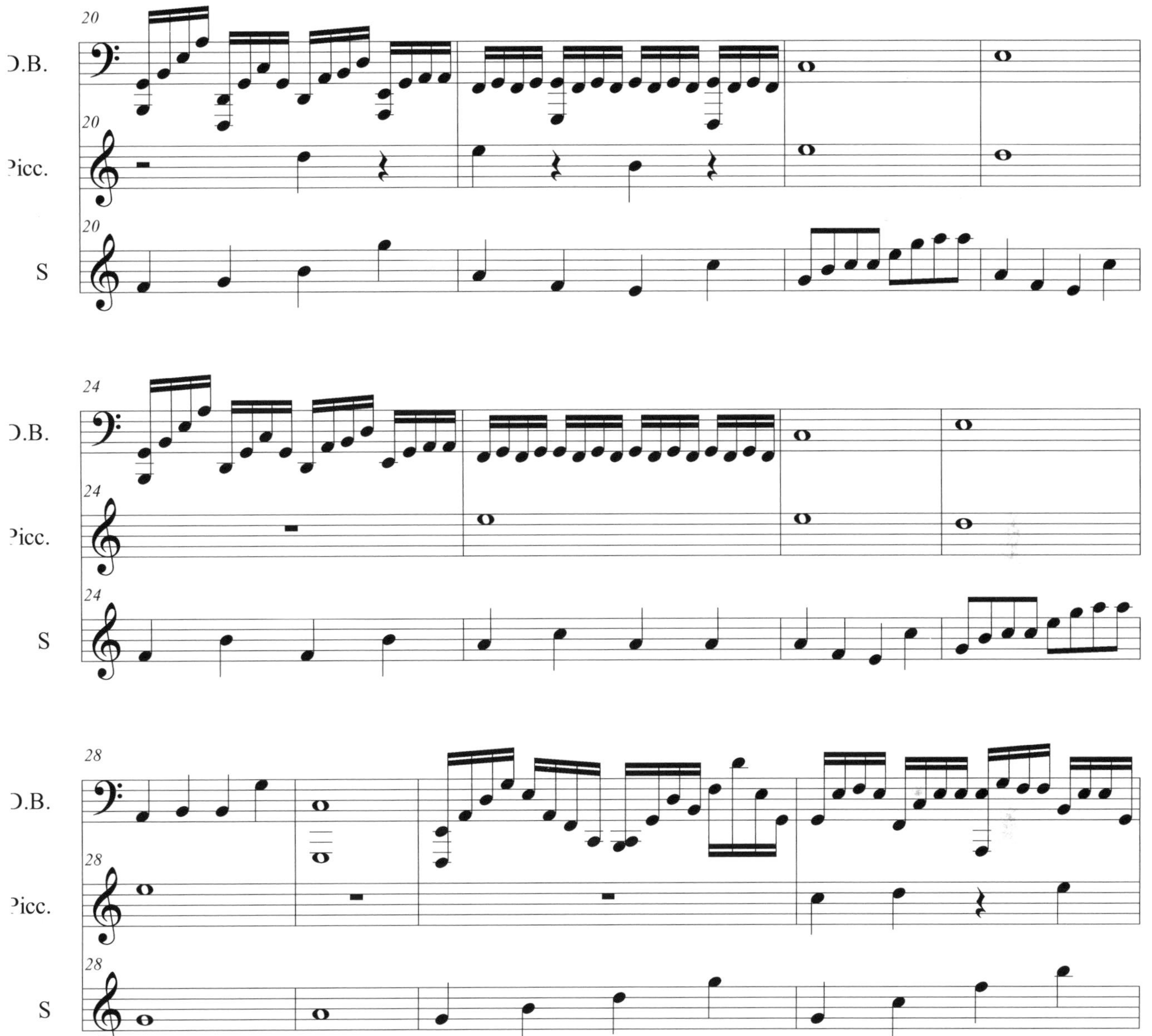
20
D.B.
Picc.
S
24
28

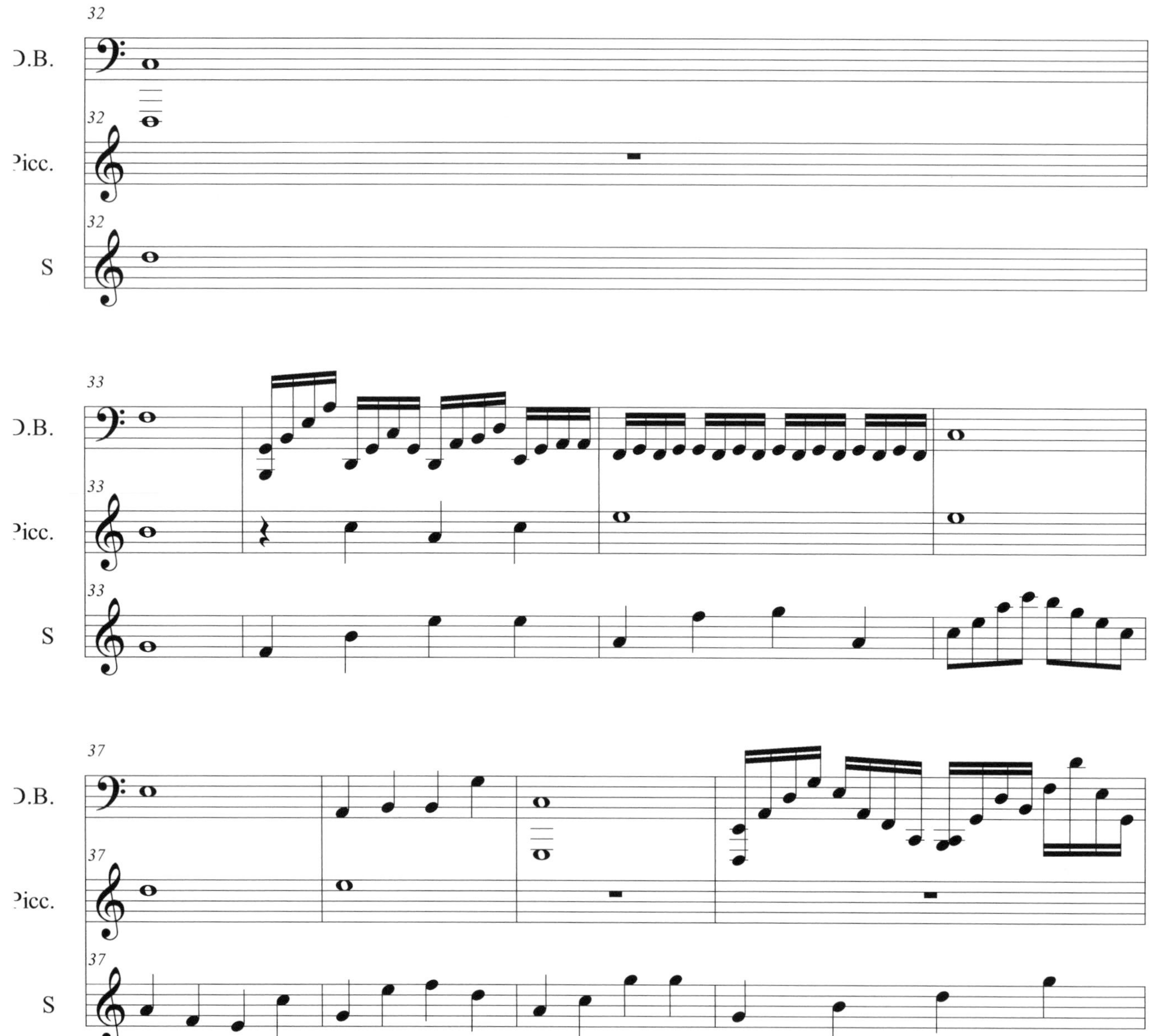
32
D.B.
32
Picc.
32
S
33
D.B.
33
Picc.
33
S
37
D.B.
37
Picc.
37
S

41
D.B.
41
Picc.
41
S
45
D.B.
45
Picc.
45
S
48
D.B.
48
Picc.
48
S

52
D.B.
Picc.
S
55
58

61
D.B.
Picc.
S
64
68

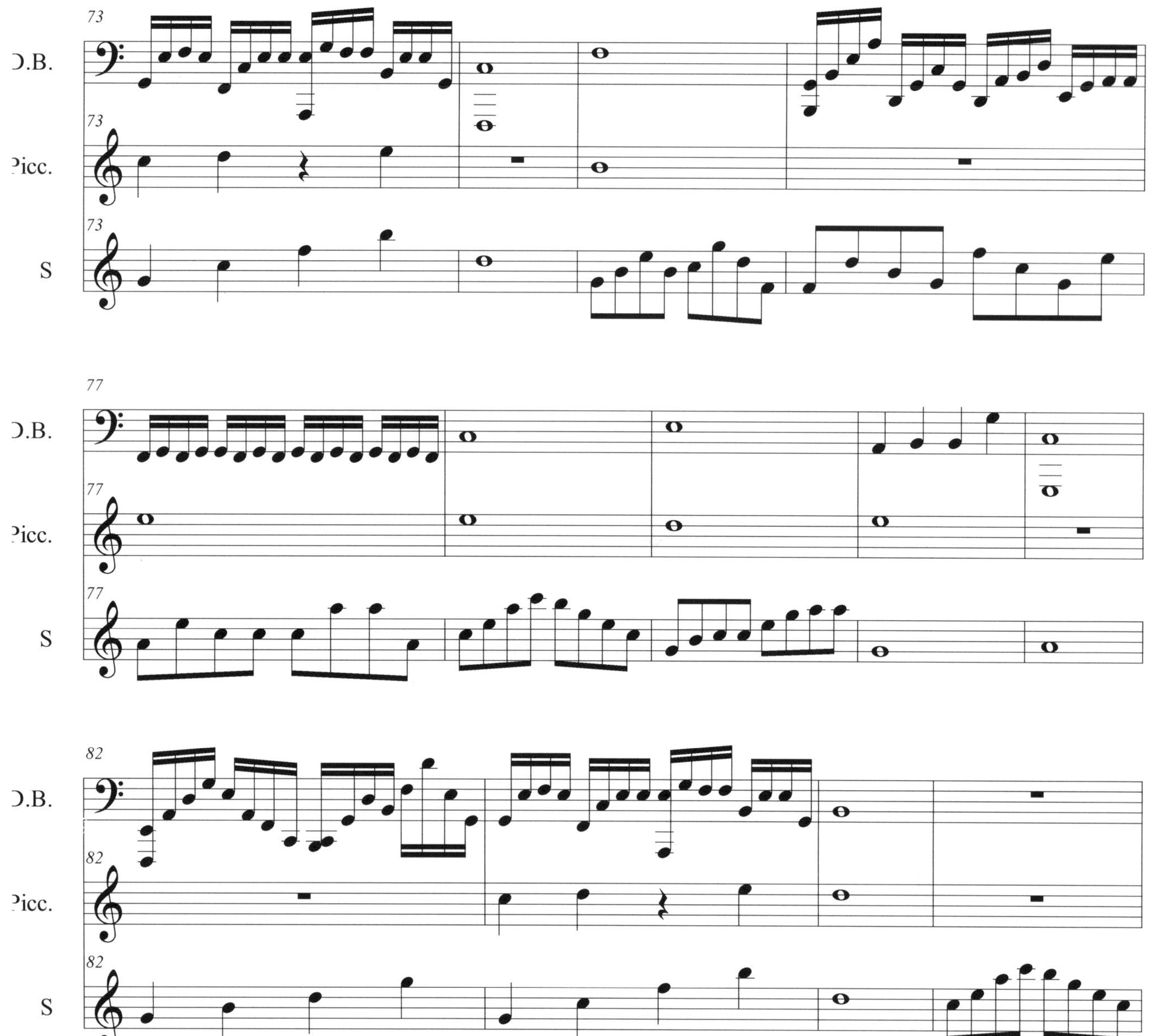
73
D.B.
73
Picc.
73
S
77
D.B.
77
Picc.
77
S
82
D.B.
82
Picc.
82
S

86
D.B.
86
Picc.
86
S
89
D.B.
89
Picc.
89
S
92
D.B.
92
Picc.
92
S

95
D.B.
Picc.
S
98
101

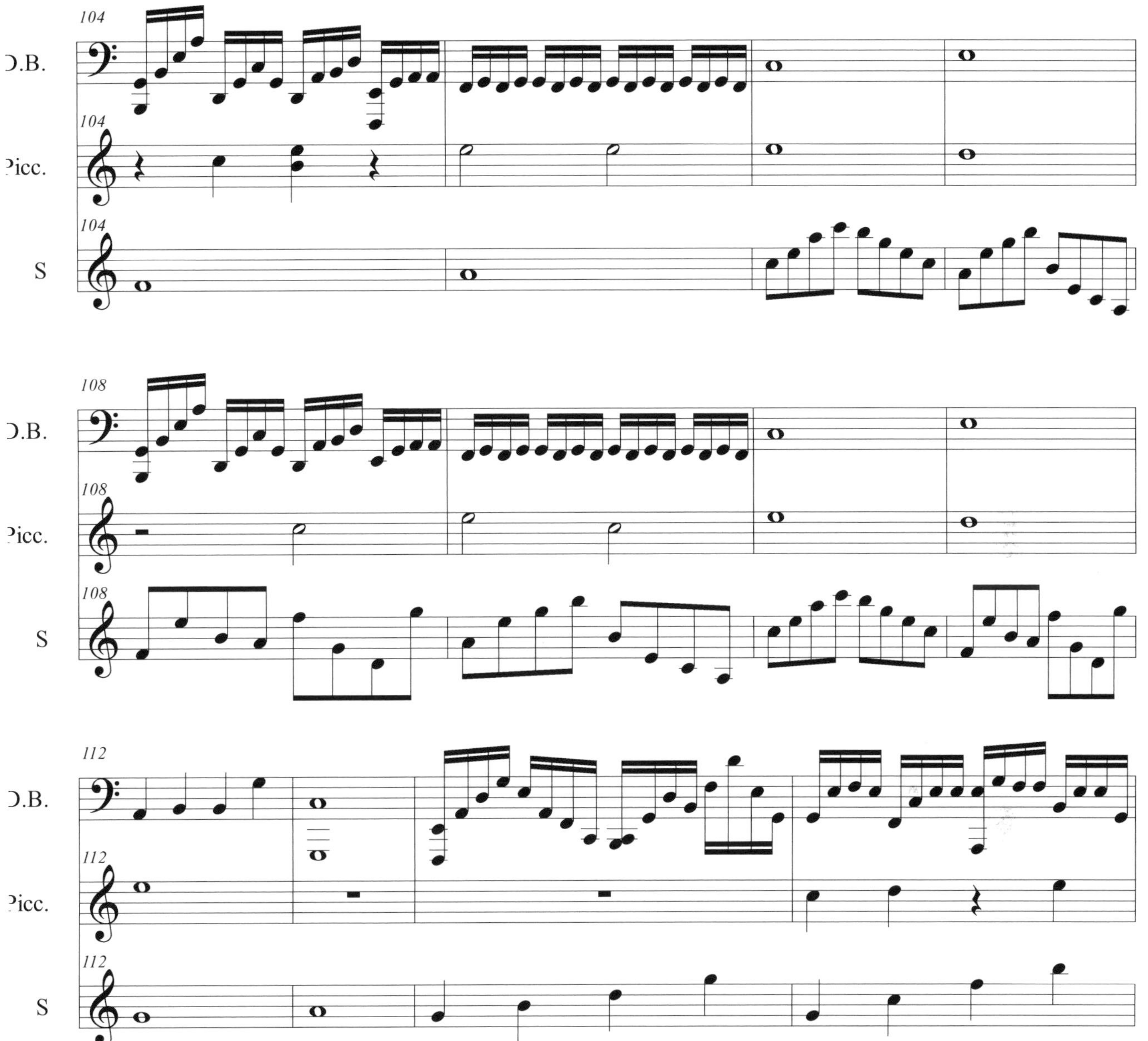
104
D.B.
Picc.
S
108
112

116
D.B.
116
Picc.
116
S
120
D.B.
120
Picc.
120
S
125
D.B.
125
Picc.
125
S

Score

Sonata No 35, Op 282 - I Am Not Angry - 2

Dr. Anis I. Milad

11
.Gtr.
ʌdn.
11
Tbn.
14
.Gtr.
ʌdn.
14
Tbn.
17
.Gtr.
ʌdn.
17
Tbn.

20
.Gtr.
Mdn.
20
Tbn.
24
.Gtr.
Mdn.
24
Tbn.
28
.Gtr.
Mdn.
28
Tbn.

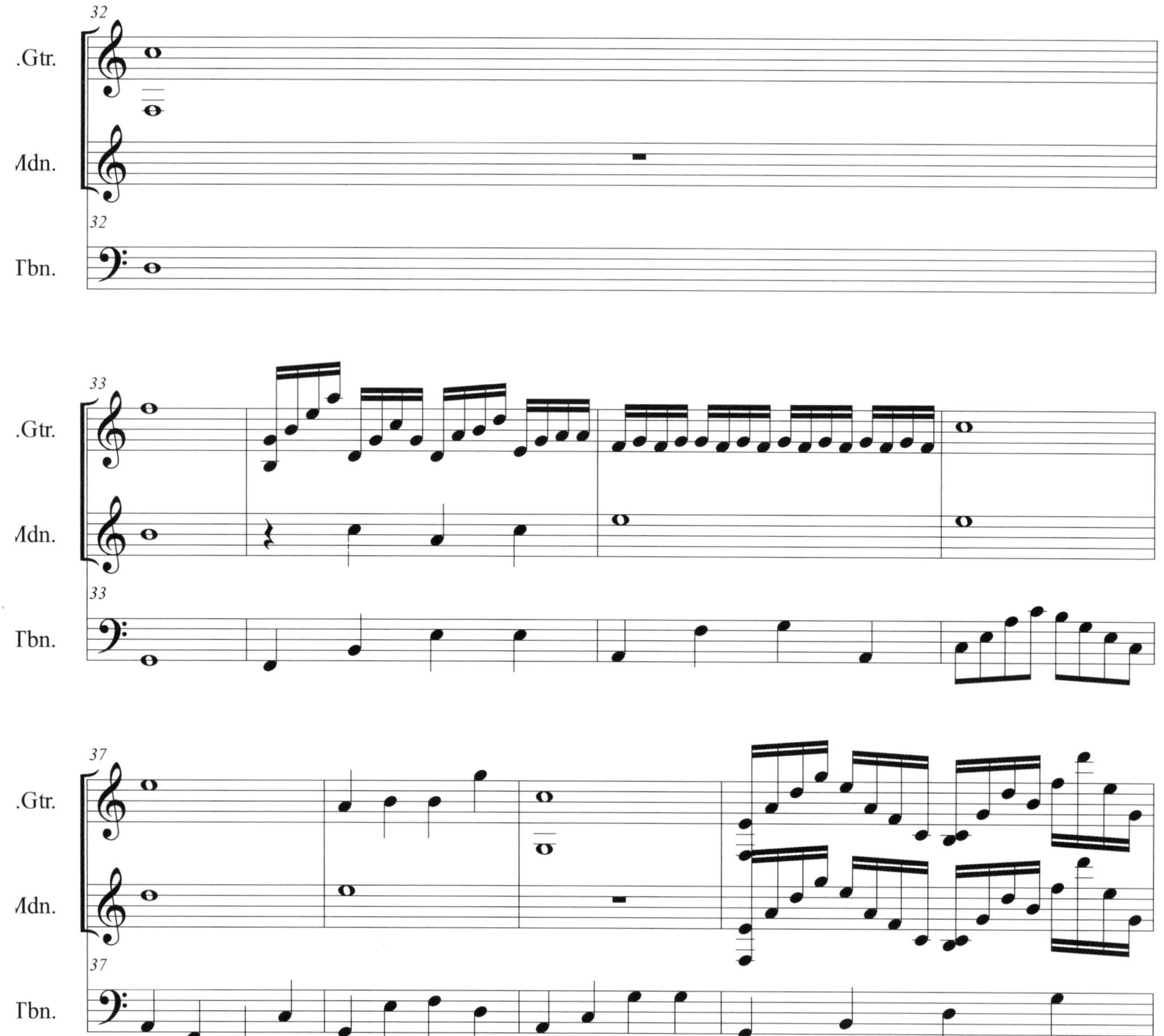
32
.Gtr.
Mdn.
32
Tbn.
33
.Gtr.
Mdn.
33
Tbn.
37
.Gtr.
Mdn.
37
Tbn.

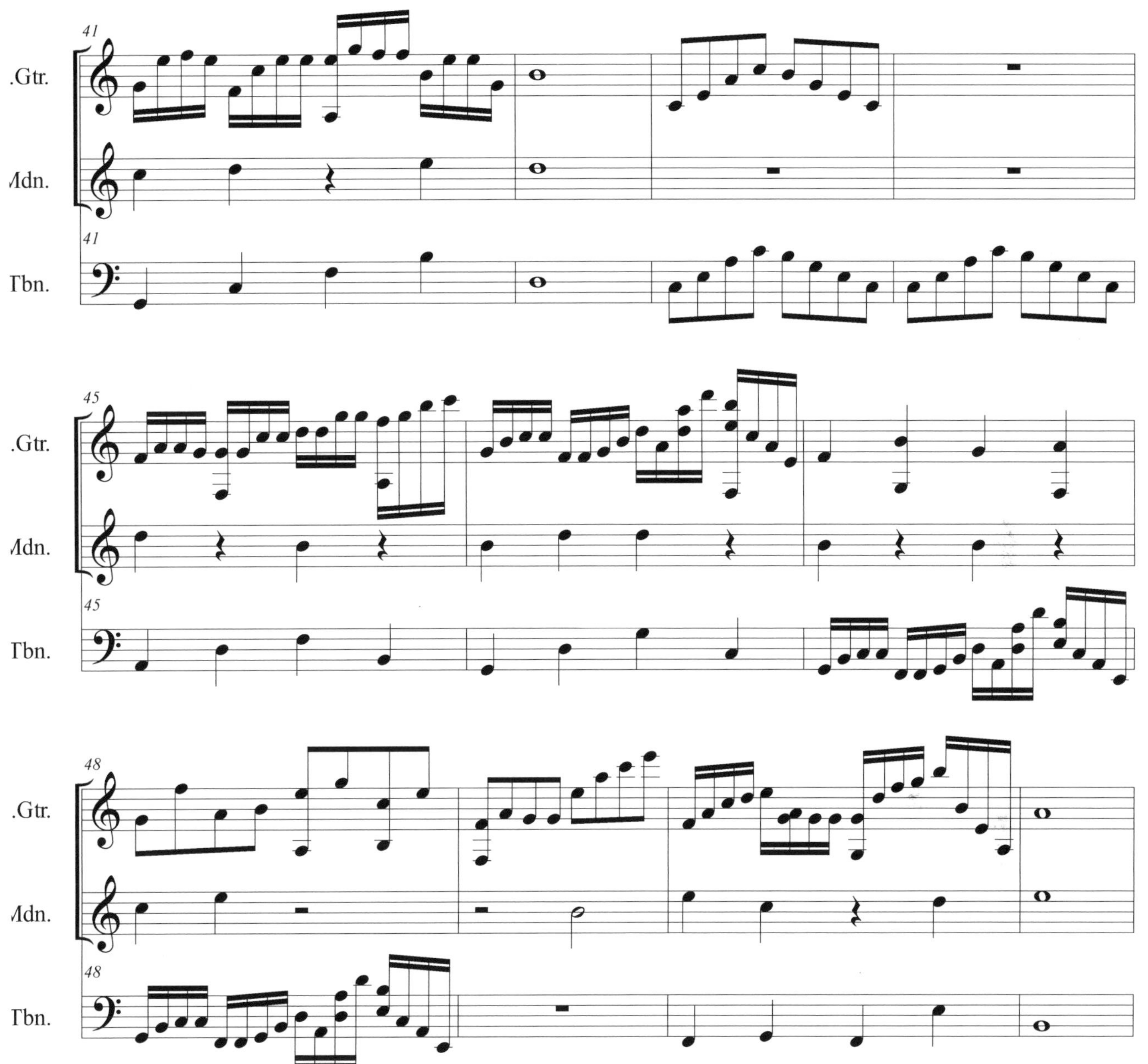
41
.Gtr.
Mdn.
41
Tbn.
45
.Gtr.
Mdn.
45
Tbn.
48
.Gtr.
Mdn.
48
Tbn.

52
.Gtr.
Mdn.
52
Tbn.
55
.Gtr.
Mdn.
55
Tbn.
58
.Gtr.
Mdn.
58
Tbn.

61
.Gtr.
Mdn.
61
Tbn.
64
.Gtr.
Mdn.
64
Tbn.
68
.Gtr.
Mdn.
68
Tbn.

73
.Gtr.
Mdn.
73
Tbn.
77
.Gtr.
Mdn.
77
Tbn.
82
.Gtr.
Mdn.
82
Tbn.

86
.Gtr.
Mdn.
86
Tbn.
89
.Gtr.
Mdn.
89
Tbn.
92
.Gtr.
Mdn.
92
Tbn.

95
.Gtr.
Mdn.
95
Tbn.
98
.Gtr.
Mdn.
98
Tbn.
101
.Gtr.
Mdn.
101
Tbn.

104
.Gtr.
Mdn.
104
Tbn.
108
.Gtr.
Mdn.
108
Tbn.
112
.Gtr.
Mdn.
112
Tbn.

116
.Gtr.
Mdn.
116
Tbn.
120
.Gtr.
Mdn.
120
Tbn.
125
.Gtr.
Mdn.
125
Tbn.

Score

Sonata No 35, Op 282 - I Am Not Angry - Part 3

Dr. Anis I. Milad

11
B
11
Str.
11
imp.
14
B
14
Str.
14
imp.
17
B
17
Str.
17
imp.

Sonata No 35, Op 282 - I Am Not Angry - Part 3

31
B
31
Str.
31
imp.
32
B
32
Str.
32
imp.
33
B
33
Str.
33
imp.

Sonata No 35, Op 282 - I Am Not Angry - Part 3

Sonata No 35, Op 282 - I Am Not Angry - Part 3

Sonata No 35, Op 282 - I Am Not Angry - Part 3

66
B
Str.
imp.
70
74

Sonata No 35, Op 282 - I Am Not Angry - Part 3

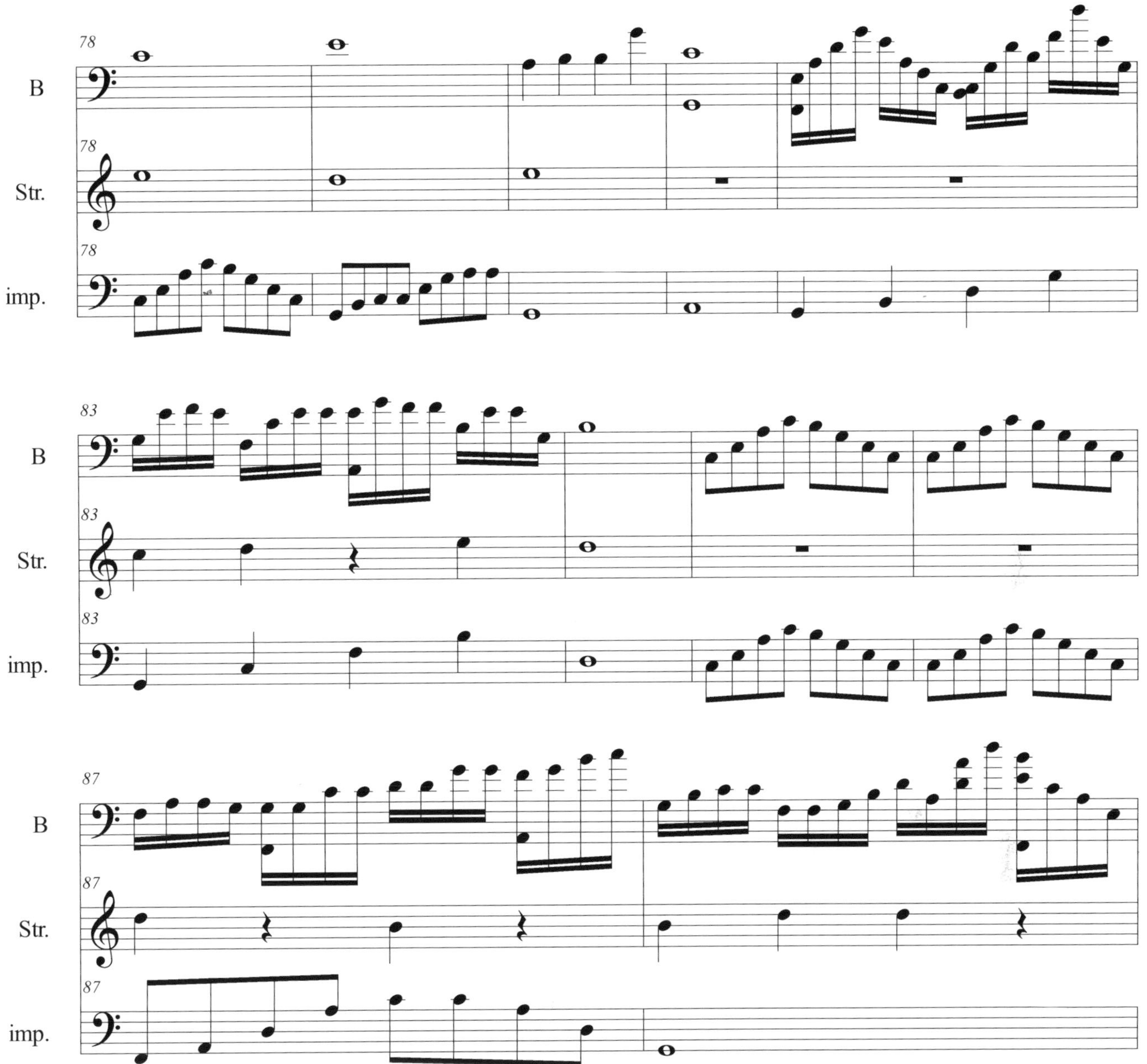

89
B
89
Str.
89
imp.
92
B
92
Str.
92
imp.
95
B
95
Str.
95
imp.

98
B
98
Str.
98
imp.
101
B
101
Str.
101
imp.
104
B
104
Str.
104
imp.

108
B
108
Str.
108
imp.
112
B
112
Str.
112
imp.
116
B
116
Str.
116
imp.

Sonata No 35, Op 282 - I Am Not Angry - Part 3

Score

Sonata No 36, Op 283 - Guided By the Holy Spirit - Part 1

Dr. Anis I. Milad

17
imp.
ezzo
Tbn.
21
26

31
imp.
31
ezzo
31
Tbn.
32
imp.
32
ezzo
32
Tbn.
37
imp.
37
ezzo
37
Tbn.

Sonata No 36, Op 283 - Guided By the Holy Spirit - Part 1

57
imp.
57
ezzo
57
Tbn.
62
imp.
62
ezzo
62
Tbn.
67
imp.
67
ezzo
67
Tbn.

72
imp.
ezzo
Tbn.
77
82

Sonata No 36, Op 283 - Guided By the Holy Spirit - Part 1

103
imp.
ezzo
Tbn.
108
113

118
imp.
118
ezzo
118
Tbn.
123
imp.
123
ezzo
123
Tbn.
128
imp.
128
ezzo
128
Tbn.

133
imp.
133
ezzo
133
Tbn.
138
imp.
138
ezzo
138
Tbn.
144
imp.
144
ezzo
144
Tbn.

149
imp.
149
ezzo
149
Tbn.
154
imp.
154
ezzo
154
Tbn.
159
imp.
159
ezzo
159
Tbn.

164
imp.
164
ezzo
164
Tbn.
169
imp.
169
ezzo
169
Tbn.
174
imp.
174
ezzo
174
Tbn.

179
imp.
179
ezzo
179
Tbn.
184
imp.
184
ezzo
184
Tbn.

Score

Sonata No 36, Op 283 - Guided By the Holy Spirit - Part 2

Dr. Anis I. Milad

17
.Gtr.
17
Tbn.
17
Mal.
21
.Gtr.
21
Tbn.
21
Mal.
26
.Gtr.
26
Tbn.
26
Mal.

Sonata No 36, Op 283 - Guided By the Holy Spirit - Part 2

42
.Gtr.
42
Tbn.
42
Mal.
48
.Gtr.
48
Tbn.
48
Mal.
52
.Gtr.
52
Tbn.
52
Mal.

57
.Gtr.
Tbn.
Mal.
62
67

72
.Gtr.
72
Tbn.
72
Mal.
77
.Gtr.
77
Tbn.
77
Mal.
82
.Gtr.
82
Tbn.
82
Mal.

Sonata No 36, Op 283 - Guided By the Holy Spirit - Part 2

103
.Gtr.
Tbn.
Mal.
108
113

Sonata No 36, Op 283 - Guided By the Holy Spirit - Part 2

133
.Gtr.
133
Tbn.
133
Mal.
138
.Gtr.
138
Tbn.
138
Mal.
144
.Gtr.
144
Tbn.
144
Mal.

149
.Gtr.
149
Tbn.
149
Mal.
154
.Gtr.
154
Tbn.
154
Mal.
159
.Gtr.
159
Tbn.
159
Mal.

164
.Gtr.
164
Tbn.
164
Mal.
169
.Gtr.
169
Tbn.
169
Mal.
174
.Gtr.
174
Tbn.
174
Mal.

Sonata No 36, Op 283 - Guided By the Holy Spirit - Part 2

Score

Sonata No 36, Op 283 - Guided By the Holy Spirit - Part 3

Dr. Anis I. Milad

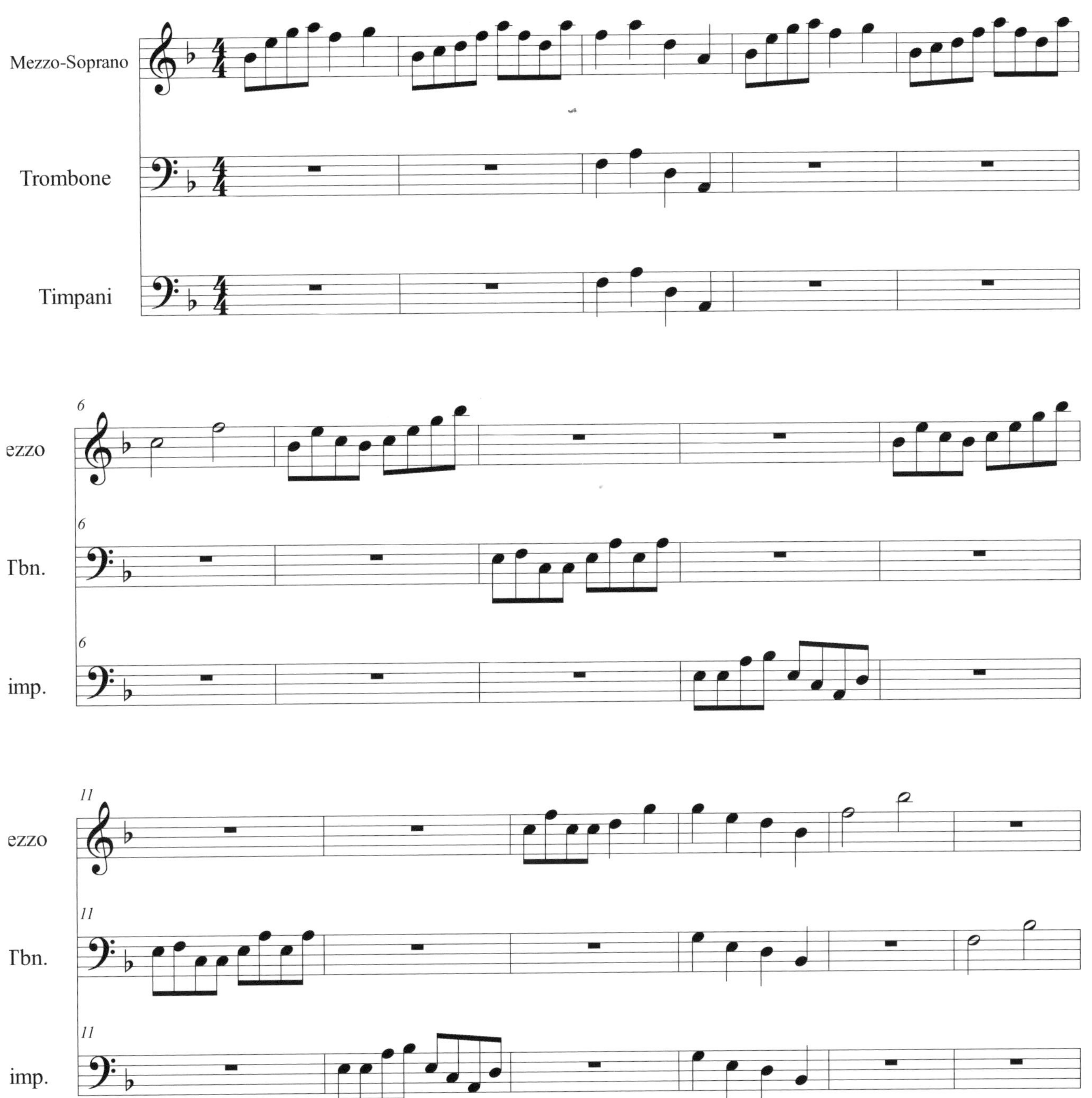

Sonata No 36, Op 283 - Guided By the Holy Spirit - Part 3

Sonata No 36, Op 283 - Guided By the Holy Spirit - Part 3

Sonata No 36, Op 283 - Guided By the Holy Spirit - Part 3

57
ezzo
57
Tbn.
57
imp.
62
ezzo
62
Tbn.
62
imp.
67
ezzo
67
Tbn.
67
imp.

72
ezzo
72
Tbn.
72
imp.
77
ezzo
77
Tbn.
77
imp.
82
ezzo
82
Tbn.
82
imp.

87
ezzo
87
Tbn.
87
imp.
92
ezzo
92
Tbn.
92
imp.
98
ezzo
98
Tbn.
98
imp.

103
ezzo
103
Tbn.
103
imp.
108
ezzo
108
Tbn.
108
imp.
113
ezzo
113
Tbn.
113
imp.

118
ezzo
118
Tbn.
118
imp.
123
ezzo
123
Tbn.
123
imp.
128
ezzo
128
Tbn.
128
imp.

133
ezzo
133
Tbn.
133
imp.
138
ezzo
138
Tbn.
138
imp.
144
ezzo
144
Tbn.
144
imp.

149
ezzo
149
Tbn.
149
imp.
154
ezzo
154
Tbn.
154
imp.
159
ezzo
159
Tbn.
159
imp.

164
ezzo
164
Tbn.
164
imp.
169
ezzo
169
Tbn.
169
imp.
174
ezzo
174
Tbn.
174
imp.

179
ezzo
179
Tbn.
179
imp.
184
ezzo
184
Tbn.
184
imp.

Score

Sonata No 37, Op 284 - Celebrating My Bleeding Heart - Part 1

Dr. Anis I. Miulad

10
Vla.
10
.Gtr.
10
Hn.
13
Vla.
13
.Gtr.
13
Hn.
18
Vla.
18
.Gtr.
18
Hn.

Sonata No 37, Op 284 - Celebrating My Bleeding Heart - Part 1

32
Vla.
32
.Gtr.
32
Hn.
33
Vla.
33
.Gtr.
33
Hn.
35
Vla.
35
.Gtr.
35
Hn.

Sonata No 37, Op 284 - Celebrating My Bleeding Heart - Part 1

50
Vla.
50
.Gtr.
50
Hn.
54
Vla.
54
.Gtr.
54
Hn.
58
Vla.
58
.Gtr.
58
Hn.

61
Vla.
61
.Gtr.
61
Hn.
65
Vla.
65
.Gtr.
65
Hn.
68
Vla.
68
.Gtr.
68
Hn.

73
Vla.
73
.Gtr.
73
Hn.
75
Vla.
75
.Gtr.
75
Hn.
79
Vla.
79
.Gtr.
79
Hn.

83
Vla.
83
.Gtr.
83
Hn.
87
Vla.
87
.Gtr.
87
Hn.
89
Vla.
89
.Gtr.
89
Hn.

92
Vla.
92
.Gtr.
92
Hn.
95
Vla.
95
.Gtr.
95
Hn.
99
Vla.
99
.Gtr.
99
Hn.

102
Vla.
102
.Gtr.
102
Hn.
106
Vla.
106
.Gtr.
106
Hn.
111
Vla.
111
.Gtr.
111
Hn.

Score

Sonata No 37, Op 284 - Celebrating My Bleeding Heart - Part 2

Dr. Anis I. Miulad

10
imp.
10
Tbn.
uph.
13
imp.
13
Tbn.
uph.
18
imp.
18
Tbn.
uph.

21
imp.
21
Tbn.
uph.
25
imp.
25
Tbn.
uph.
29
imp.
29
Tbn.
uph.

32
imp.
32
Tbn.
uph.
33
imp.
33
Tbn.
uph.
35
imp.
35
Tbn.
uph.

38
imp.
38
Tbn.
uph.
43
imp.
43
Tbn.
uph.
46
imp.
46
Tbn.
uph.

50
imp.
50
Tbn.
uph.
54
imp.
54
Tbn.
uph.
58
imp.
58
Tbn.
uph.

61
imp.
61
Tbn.
uph.
65
imp.
65
Tbn.
uph.
68
imp.
68
Tbn.
uph.

Sonata No 37, Op 284 - Celebrating My Bleeding Heart - Part 2

Sonata No 37, Op 284 - Celebrating My Bleeding Heart - Part 2

93
imp.
93
Tbn.
uph.
98
imp.
98
Tbn.
uph.
101
imp.
101
Tbn.
uph.

Sonata No 37, Op 284 - Celebrating My Bleeding Heart - Part 2

Score

Sonata No 37, Op 284 - Celebrating My Bleeding Heart - Part 3

Dr. Anis I. Miulad

Sonata No 37, Op 284 - Celebrating My Bleeding Heart - Part 3

20
Hn.
20
D.B.
20
Mdn.
24
Hn.
24
D.B.
24
Mdn.
28
Hn.
28
D.B.
28
Mdn.

32
Hn.
32
D.B.
32
Mdn.
33
Hn.
33
D.B.
33
Mdn.
35
Hn.
35
D.B.
35
Mdn.

Sonata No 37, Op 284 - Celebrating My Bleeding Heart - Part 3

50
Hn.
50
D.B.
50
Mdn.
54
Hn.
54
D.B.
54
Mdn.
58
Hn.
58
D.B.
58
Mdn.

Sonata No 37, Op 284 - Celebrating My Bleeding Heart - Part 3

73
Hn.
73
D.B.
73
Mdn.
75
Hn.
75
D.B.
75
Mdn.
79
Hn.
79
D.B.
79
Mdn.

83
Hn.
83
D.B.
83
Mdn.
87
Hn.
87
D.B.
87
Mdn.
89
Hn.
89
D.B.
89
Mdn.

92
Hn.
92
).B.
92
ldn.
95
Hn.
95
).B.
95
ldn.
99
Hn.
99
).B.
99
ldn.

Sonata No 37, Op 284 - Celebrating My Bleeding Heart - Part 3

Score

Symphony No 1, Op 24, in C Major

Dr. Anis I. Milad

5
Pno.
Vla.
E.B.
Perc.
9

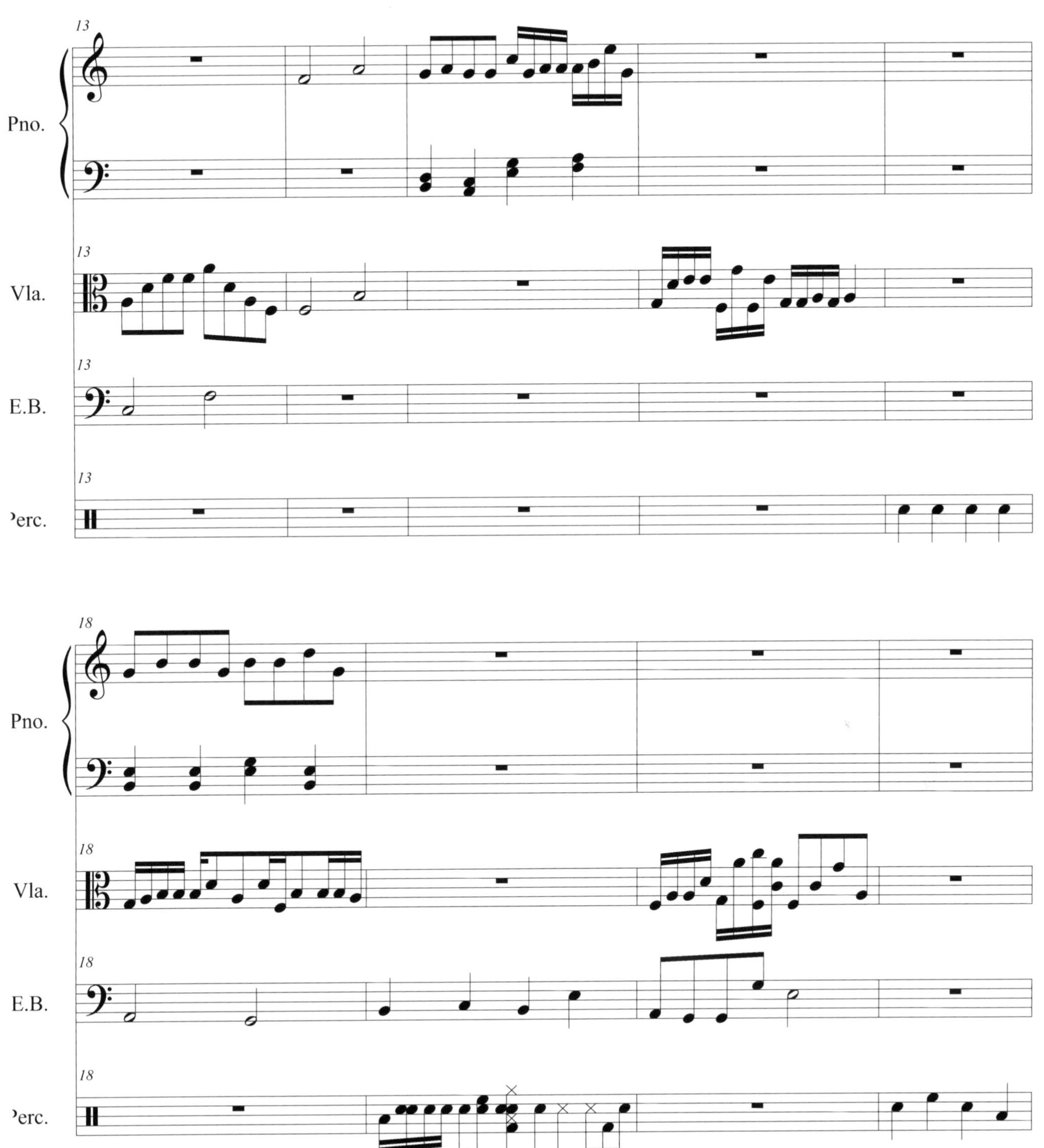
13
Pno.
Vla.
E.B.
Perc.
18
Pno.
Vla.
E.B.
Perc.

22
Pno.
Vla.
E.B.
Perc.
26
Pno.
Vla.
E.B.
Perc.

Symphony No 1, Op 24, in C Major

36
Pno.
Vla.
E.B.
Perc.
39

43
Pno.
Vla.
E.B.
Perc.
47
Pno.
Vla.
E.B.
Perc.

52
Pno.
Vla.
E.B.
Perc.
55

59
Pno.
Vla.
E.B.
Perc.
63

67
Pno.
Vla.
E.B.
Perc.
71
Pno.
Vla.
E.B.
Perc.

76
Pno.
Vla.
E.B.
Perc.
80
Pno.
Vla.
E.B.
Perc.

86
Pno.
Vla.
E.B.
Perc.
92

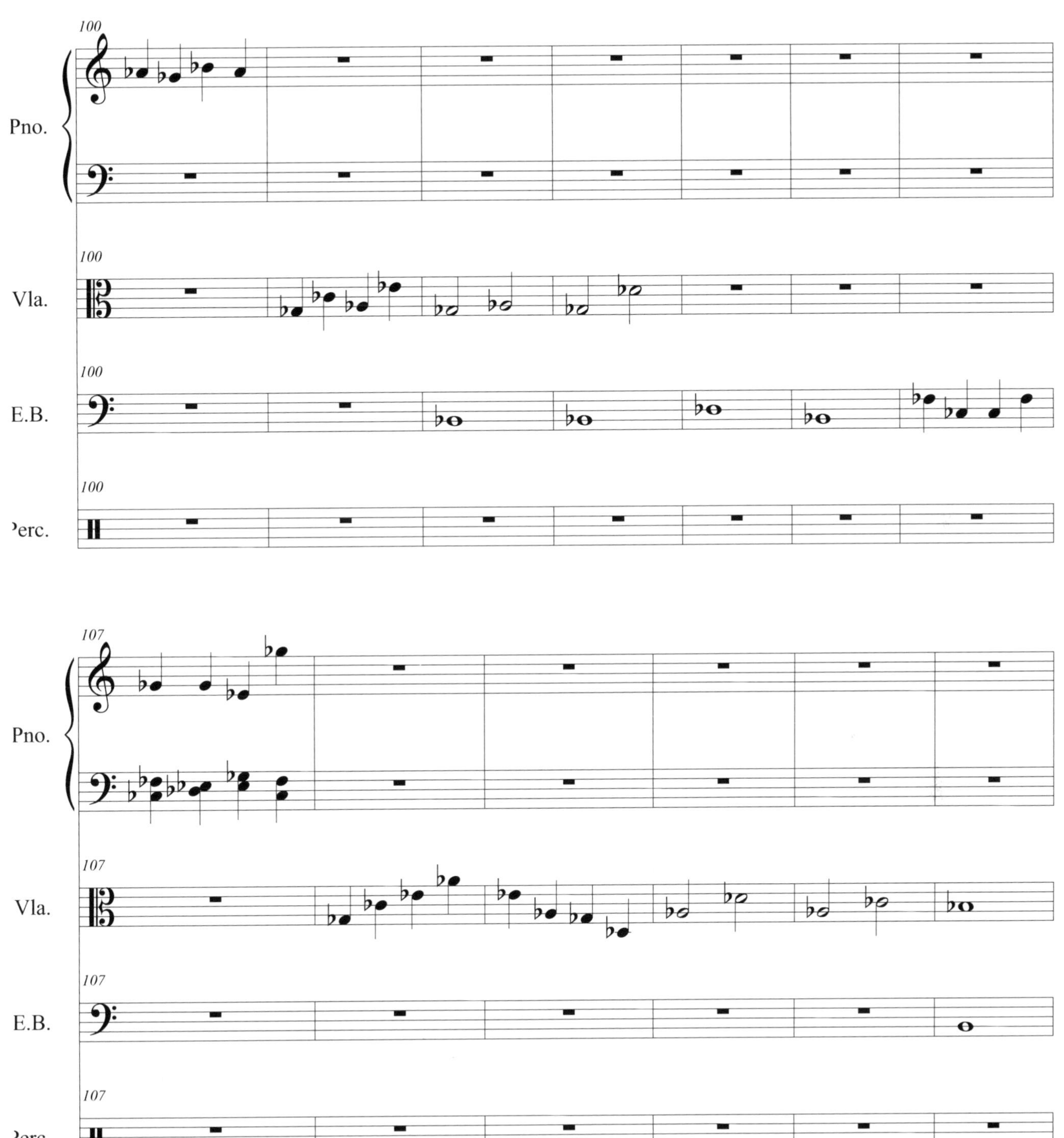
100
Pno.
Vla.
E.B.
Perc.
107
Pno.
Vla.
E.B.
Perc.

113
Pno.
113
Vla.
113
E.B.
113
Perc.
120
Pno.
120
Vla.
120
E.B.
120
Perc.

127
Pno.
Vla.
E.B.
Perc.
133

141
Pno.
141
Vla.
141
E.B.
141
Perc.
148
Pno.
148
Vla.
148
E.B.
148
Perc.

Symphony No 1, Op 24, in C Major

168
Pno.
168
Vla.
168
E.B.
168
Perc.
174
Pno.
174
Vla.
174
E.B.
174
Perc.

182
Pno.
182
Vla.
182
E.B.
182
Perc.
189
Pno.
189
Vla.
189
E.B.
189
Perc.

195
Pno.
195
Vla.
195
E.B.
195
Perc.
202
Pno.
202
Vla.
202
E.B.
202
Perc.

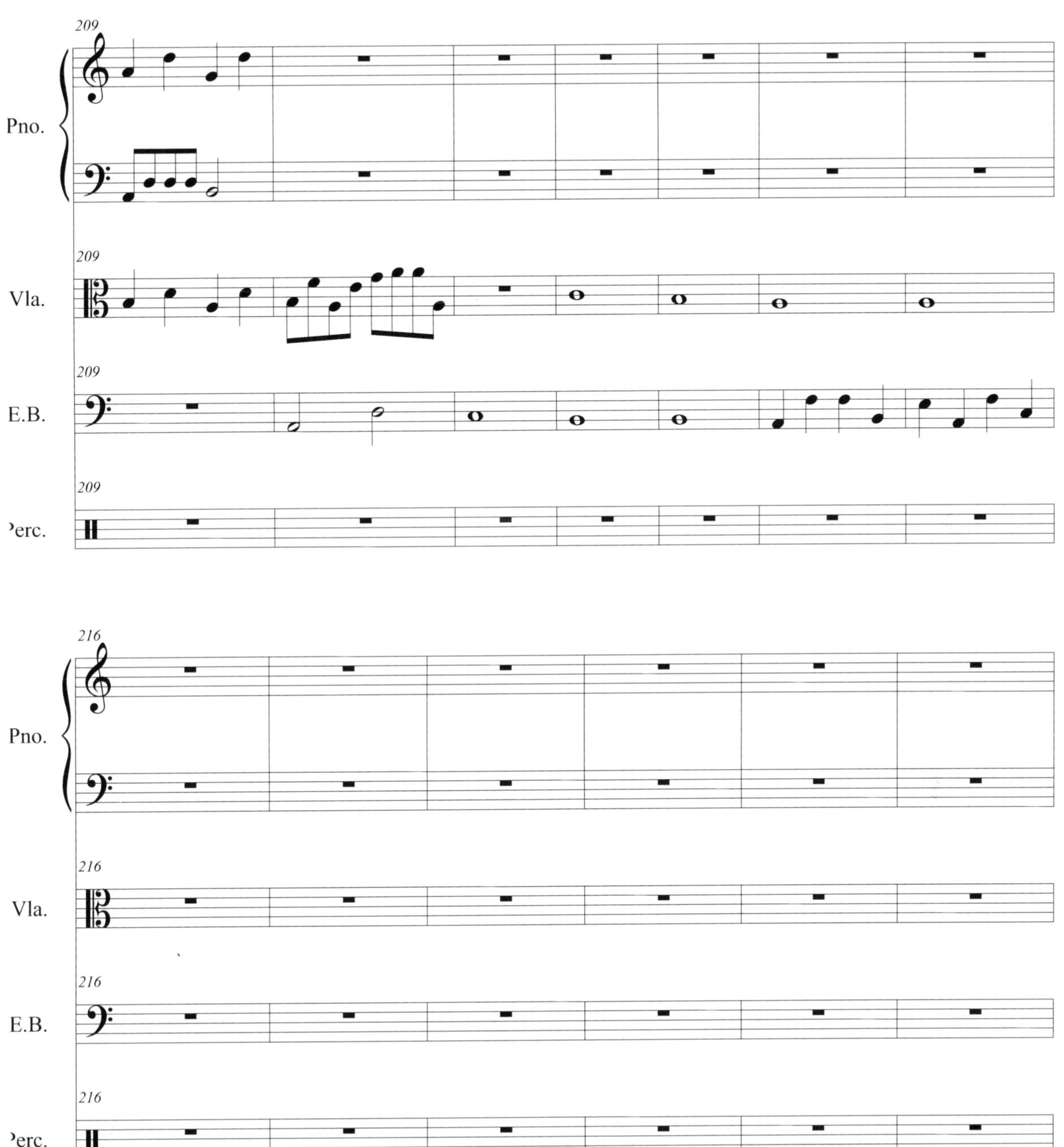
209
Pno.
209
Vla.
209
E.B.
209
Perc.
216
Pno.
216
Vla.
216
E.B.
216
Perc.

222
Pno.
222
Vla.
222
E.B.
222
Perc.
227
Pno.
227
Vla.
227
E.B.
227
Perc.

232
Pno.
Vla.
E.B.
Perc.
237

242
Pno.
242
Vla.
242
E.B.
242
Perc.
247
Pno.
247
Vla.
247
E.B.
247
Perc.

252
Pno.
Vla.
E.B.
Perc.
257

262
Pno.
262
Vla.
262
E.B.
262
Perc.
267
Pno.
267
Vla.
267
E.B.
267
Perc.

272
Pno.
272
Vla.
272
E.B.
272
Perc.
277
Pno.
277
Vla.
277
E.B.
277
Perc.

282
Pno.
282
Vla.
282
E.B.
282
Perc.
287
Pno.
287
Vla.
287
E.B.
287
Perc.

292
Pno.
292
Vla.
292
E.B.
292
Perc.
297
Pno.
297
Vla.
297
E.B.
297
Perc.

302
Pno.
302
Vla.
302
E.B.
302
Perc.
307
Pno.
307
Vla.
307
E.B.
307
Perc.

312
Pno.
312
Vla.
312
E.B.
312
Perc.
317
Pno.
317
Vla.
317
E.B.
317
Perc.

322
Pno.
322
Vla.
322
E.B.
322
Perc.
327
Pno.
327
Vla.
327
E.B.
327
Perc.

332
Pno.
Vla.
E.B.
Perc.
337

342
Pno.
342
Vla.
342
E.B.
342
Perc.
346
Pno.
346
Vla.
346
E.B.
346
Perc.

350
Pno.
350
Vla.
350
E.B.
350
Perc.
354
Pno.
354
Vla.
354
E.B.
354
Perc.

358
Pno.
358
Vla.
358
E.B.
358
Perc.
361
Pno.
361
Vla.
361
E.B.
361
Perc.

365
Pno.
Vla.
E.B.
Perc.
369

372
Pno.
372
Vla.
372
E.B.
372
Perc.
375
Pno.
375
Vla.
375
E.B.
375
Perc.

378
Pno.
Vla.
E.B.
Perc.
382

386
Pno.
Vla.
E.B.
Perc.
389

393
Pno.
Vla.
E.B.
Perc.
396

400
Pno.
Vla.
E.B.
Perc.
404

408
Pno.
408
Vla.
408
E.B.
408
Perc.
412
Pno.
412
Vla.
412
E.B.
412
Perc.

417
Pno.
Vla.
E.B.
Perc.

Score

Symphony No 2, Op 36, in C Minor

Dr. Anis I. Milad

7
Vla.
7
Picc.
Fl.
7
Vln.
10
Vla.
10
Picc.
Fl.
10
Vln.

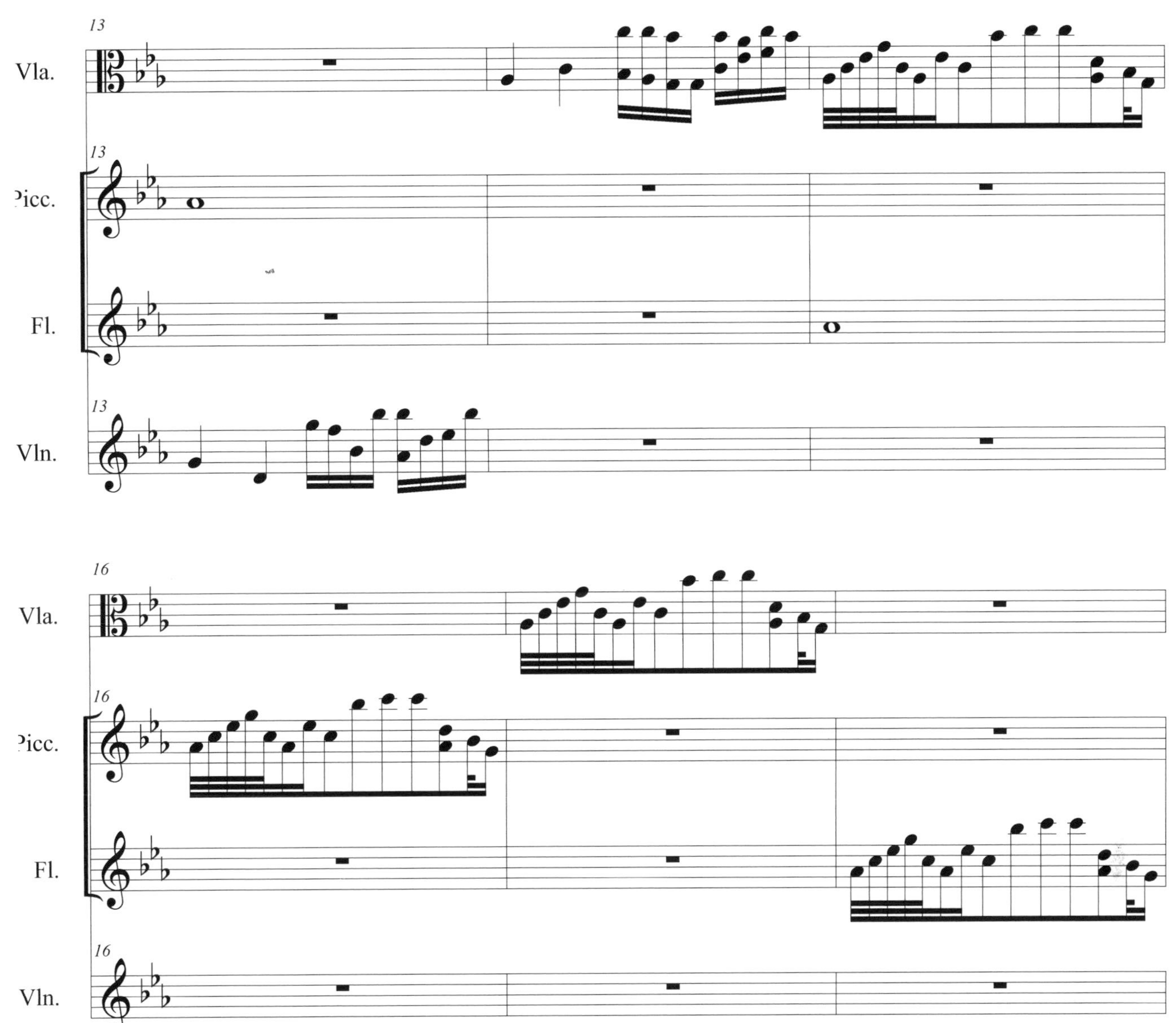
13
Vla.
13
Picc.
Fl.
13
Vln.
16
Vla.
16
Picc.
Fl.
16
Vln.

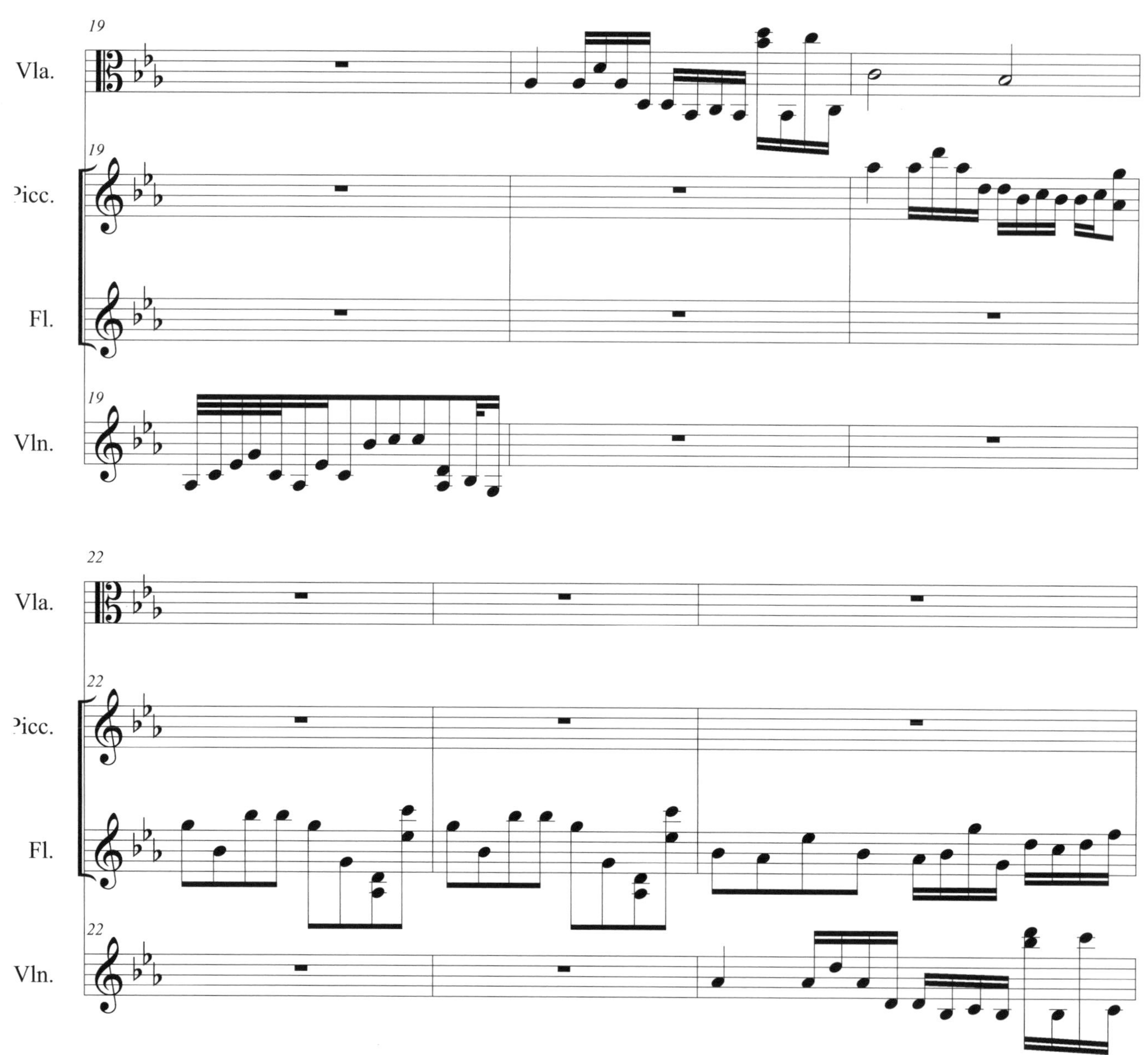
19
Vla.
19
Picc.
Fl.
19
Vln.
22
Vla.
22
Picc.
Fl.
22
Vln.

25
Vla.
25
Picc.
Fl.
25
Vln.
28
Vla.
28
Picc.
Fl.
28
Vln.

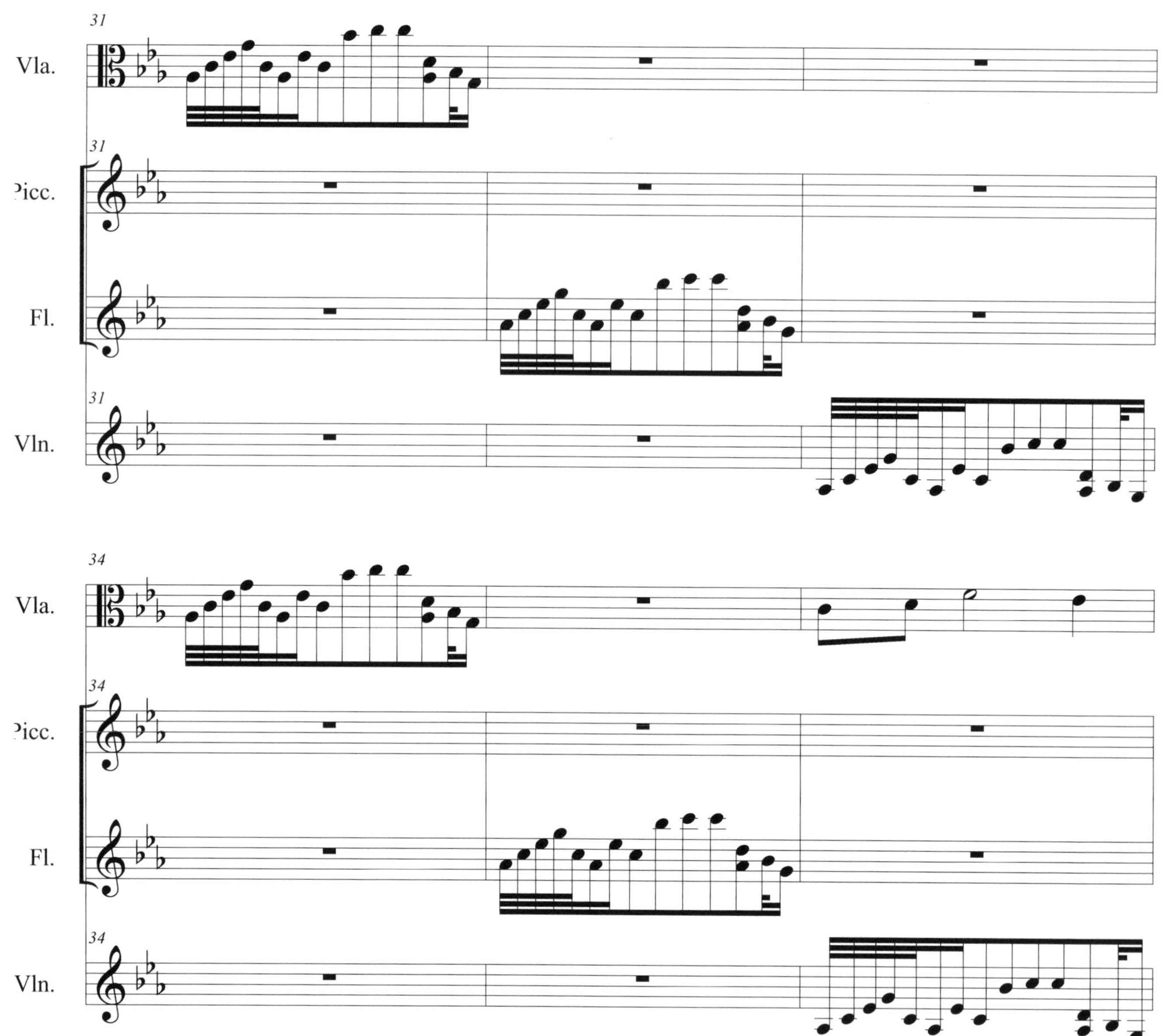
31
Vla.
31
Picc.
Fl.
31
Vln.
34
Vla.
34
Picc.
Fl.
34
Vln.

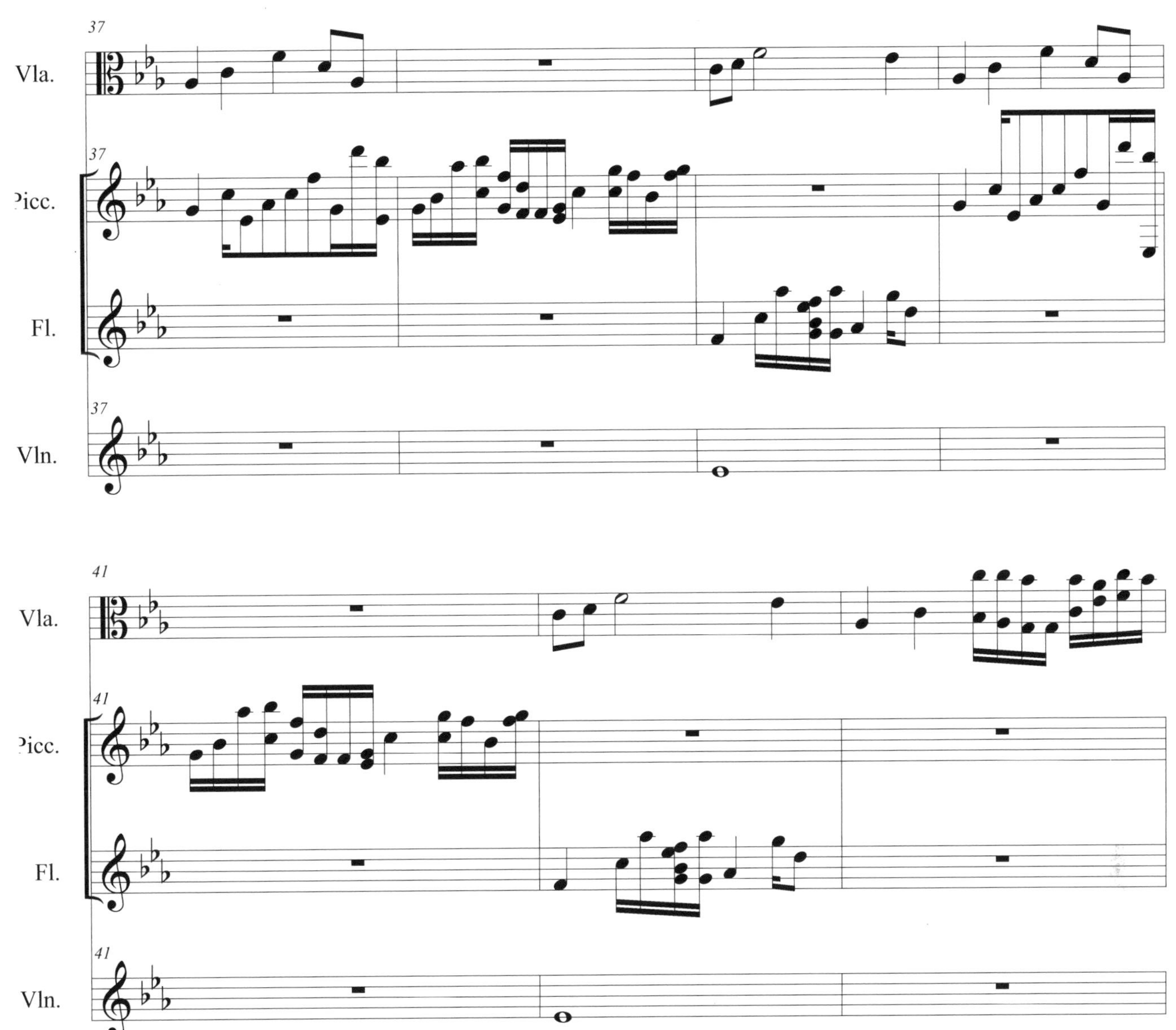
37
Vla.
Picc.
Fl.
Vln.
41

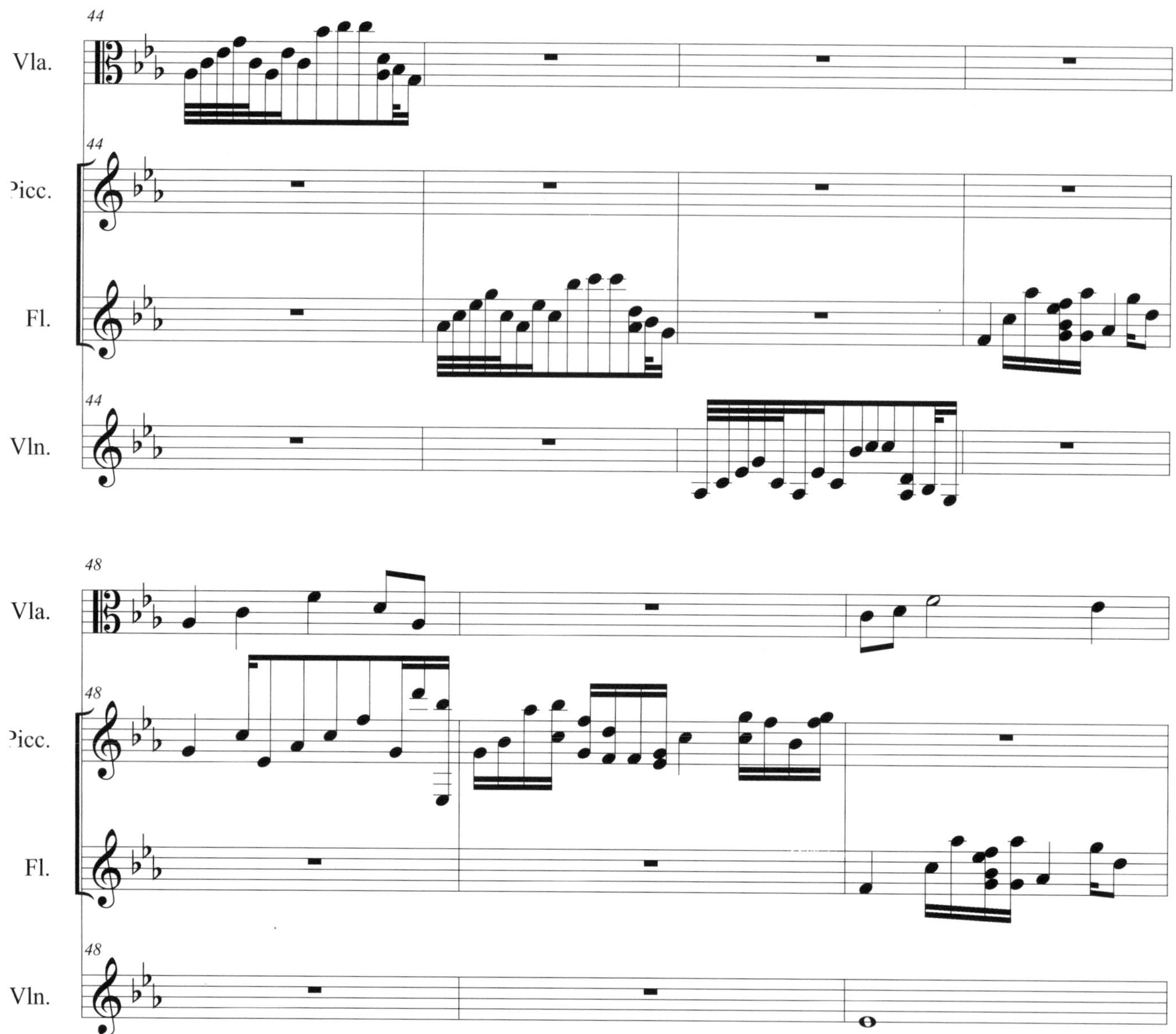
44
Vla.
44
Picc.
Fl.
44
Vln.
48
Vla.
48
Picc.
Fl.
48
Vln.

51
Vla.
51
Picc.
Fl.
51
Vln.
54
Vla.
54
Picc.
Fl.
54
Vln.

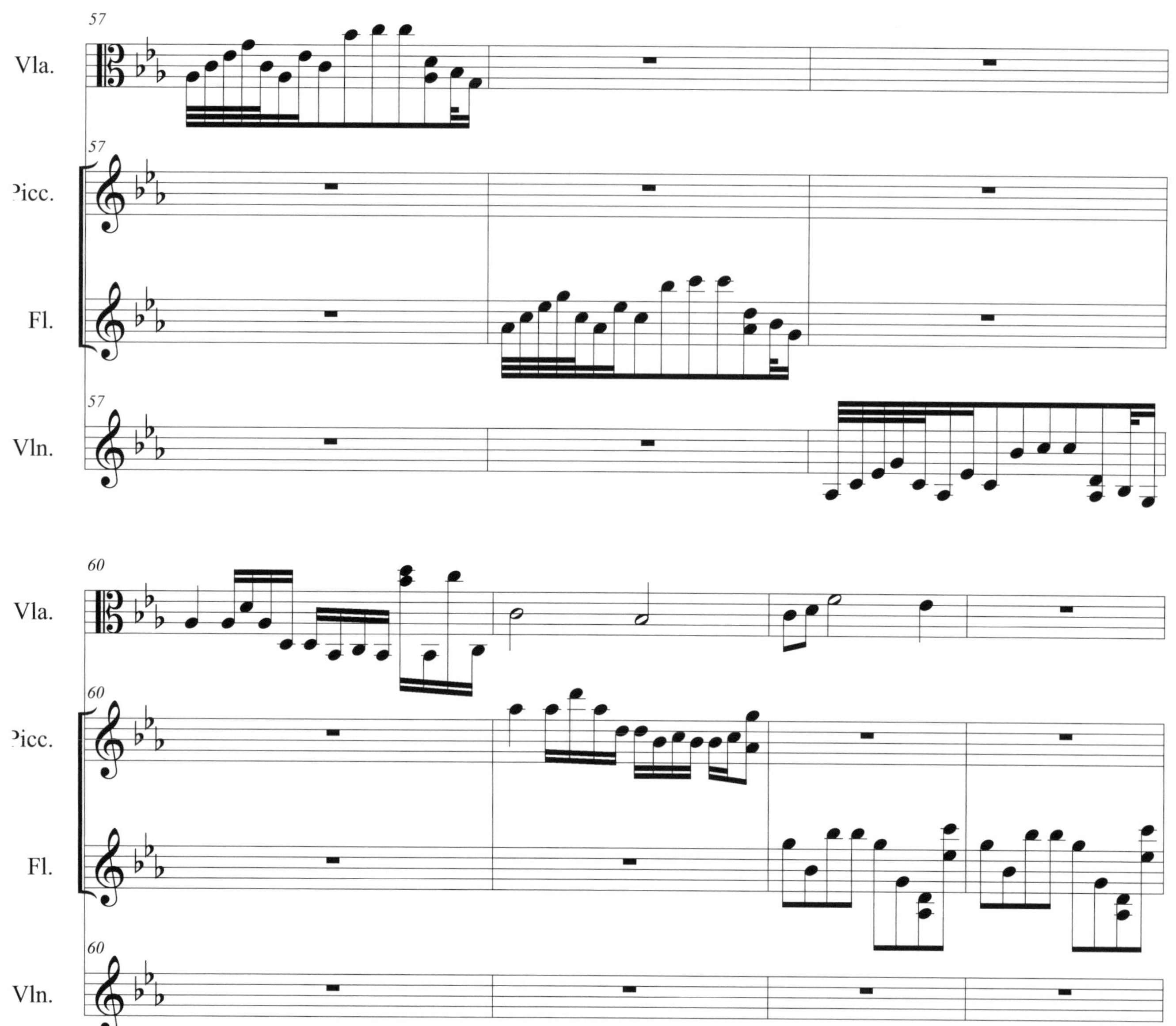
57
Vla.
57
Picc.
Fl.
57
Vln.
60
Vla.
60
Picc.
Fl.
60
Vln.

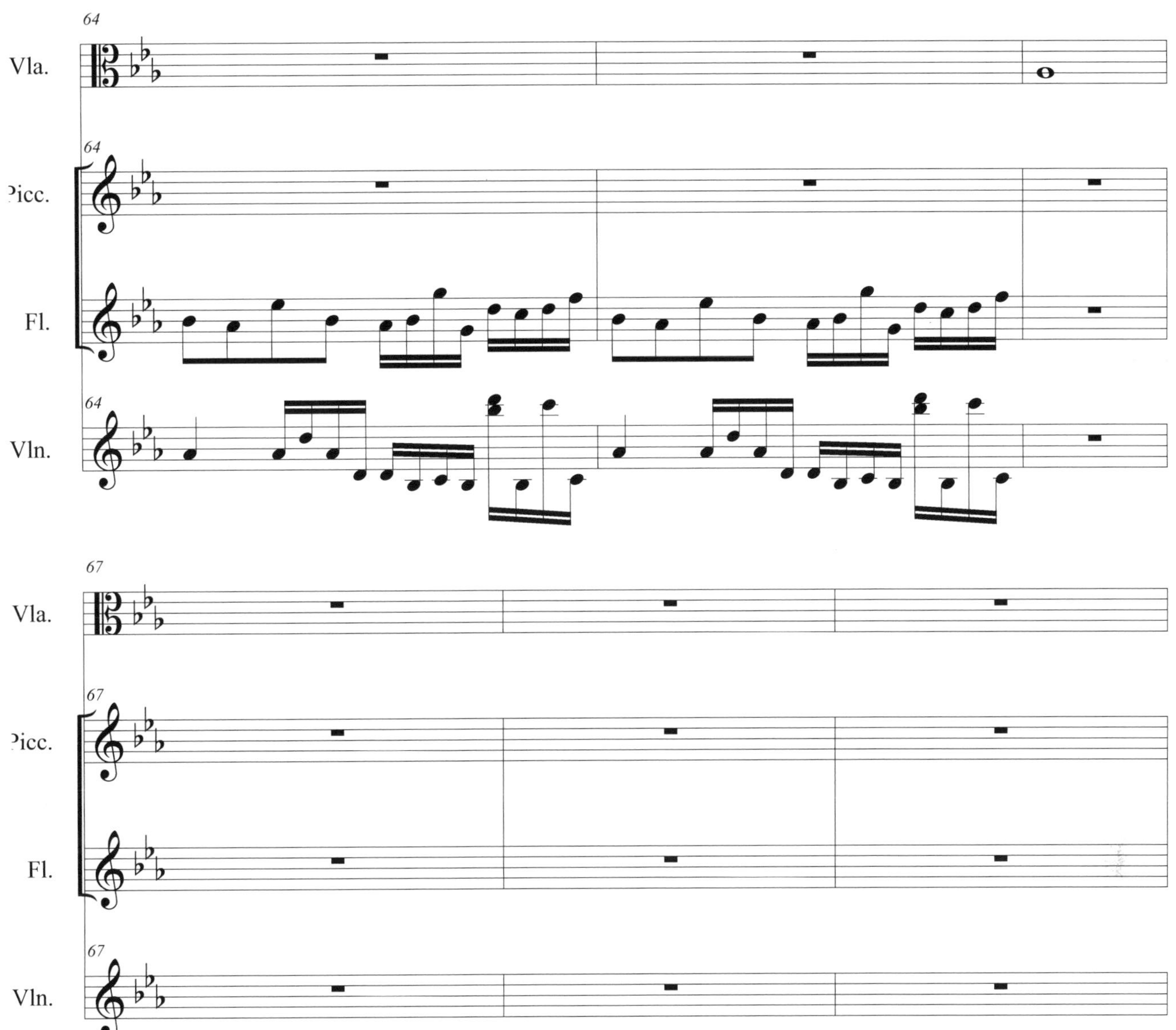
64
Vla.
Picc.
Fl.
Vln.
67

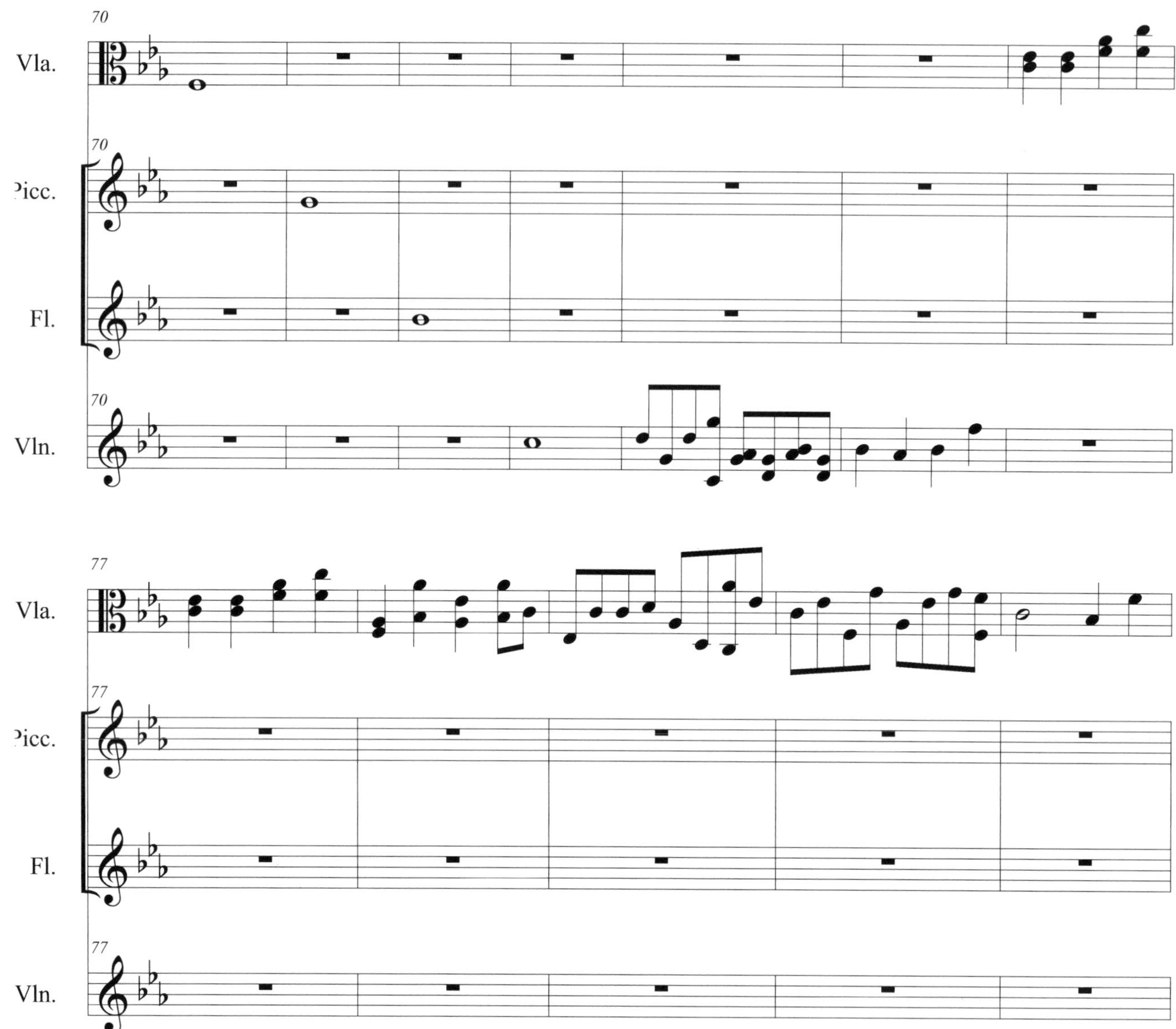
70
Vla.
70
Picc.
Fl.
70
Vln.
77
Vla.
77
Picc.
Fl.
77
Vln.

82
Vla.
82
Picc.
Fl.
82
Vln.
87
Vla.
87
Picc.
Fl.
87
Vln.

92
Vla.
92
Picc.
Fl.
92
Vln.
97
Vla.
97
Picc.
Fl.
97
Vln.

Symphony No 2, Op 36, in C Minor

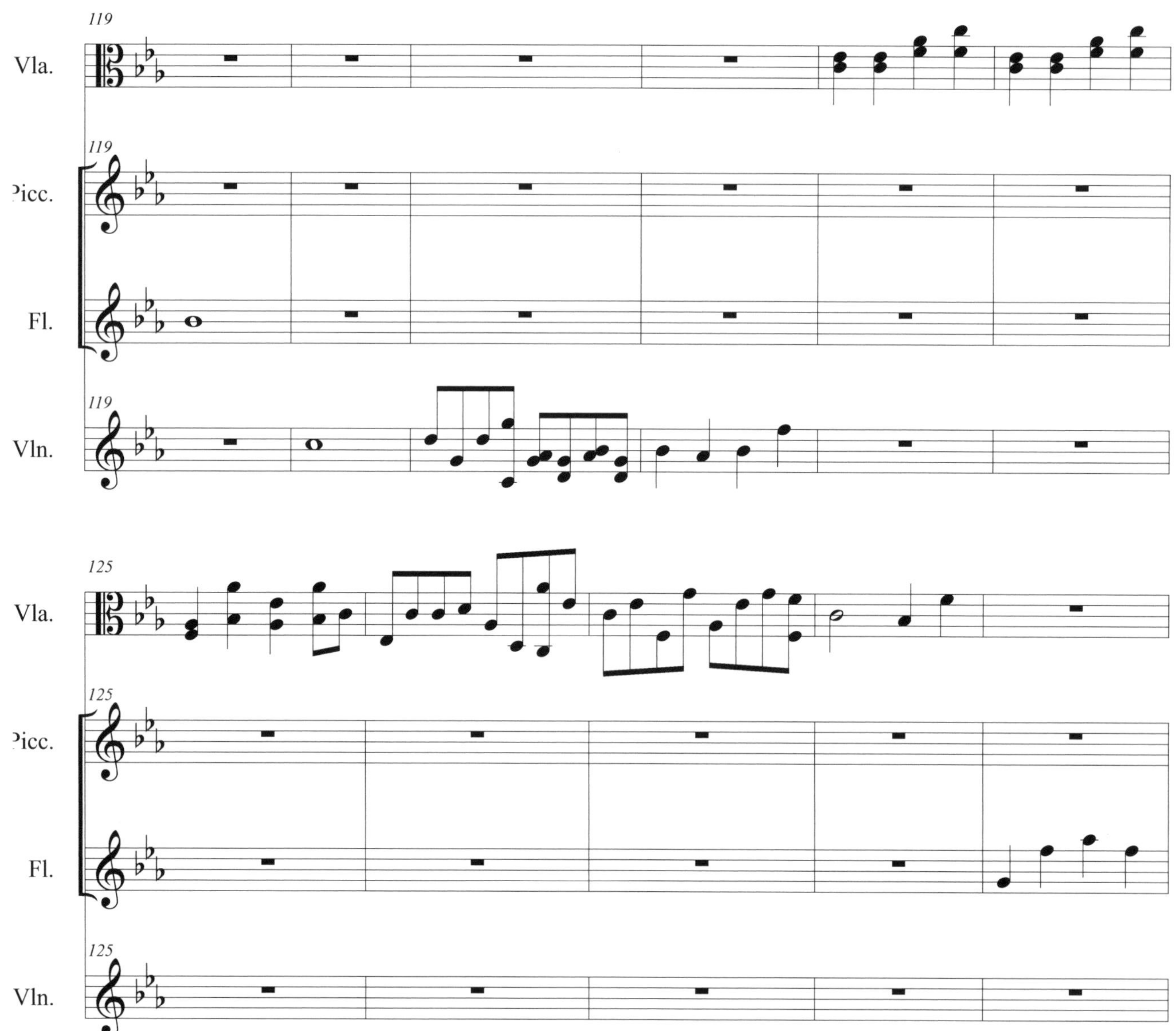
119
Vla.
119
Picc.
Fl.
119
Vln.
125
Vla.
125
Picc.
Fl.
125
Vln.

Symphony No 2, Op 36, in C Minor

140
Vla.
140
Picc.
Fl.
140
Vln.
146
Vla.
146
Picc.
Fl.
146
Vln.

153
Vla.
153
Picc.
Fl.
153
Vln.
161
Vla.
161
Picc.
Fl.
161
Vln.

167
Vla.
167
Picc.
Fl.
167
Vln.
172
Vla.
172
Picc.
Fl.
172
Vln.

177
Vla.
177
Picc.
Fl.
177
Vln.
182
Vla.
182
Picc.
Fl.
182
Vln.

Symphony No 2, Op 36, in C Minor

Symphony No 2, Op 36, in C Minor

214
Vla.
214
Picc.
Fl.
214
Vln.
217
Vla.
217
Picc.
Fl.
217
Vln.

222
Vla.
222
Picc.
Fl.
222
Vln.
228
Vla.
228
Picc.
Fl.
228
Vln.

235
Vla.
235
Picc.
Fl.
235
Vln.
238
Vla.
238
Picc.
Fl.
238
Vln.

243
Vla.
243
Picc.
Fl.
243
Vln.
249
Vla.
249
Picc.
Fl.
249
Vln.

256
Vla.
256
Picc.
Fl.
256
Vln.
259
Vla.
259
Picc.
Fl.
259
Vln.

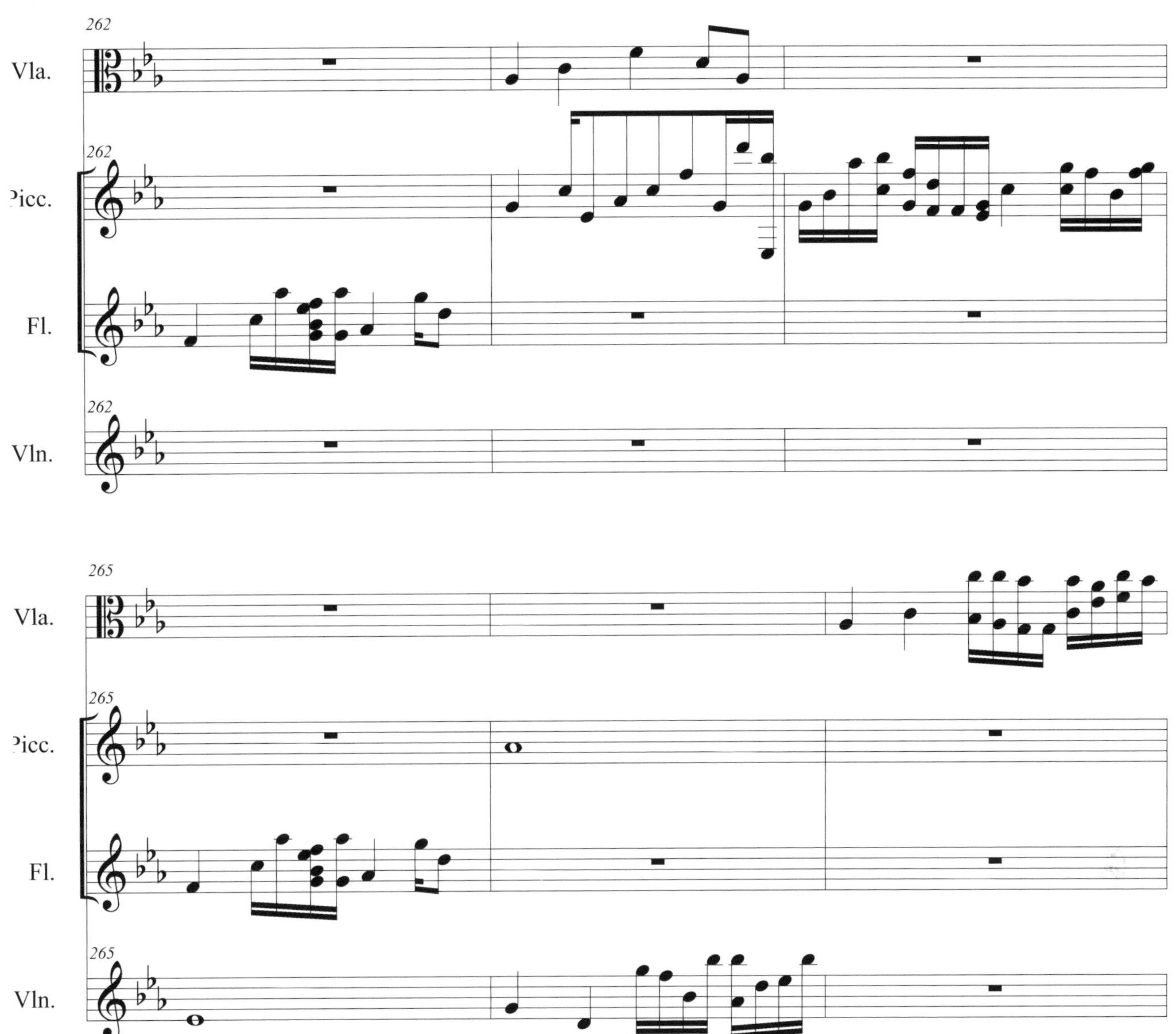
262
Vla.
262
Picc.
Fl.
262
Vln.
265
Vla.
265
Picc.
Fl.
265
Vln.

268
Vla.
268
Picc.
Fl.
268
Vln.
271
Vla.
271
Picc.
Fl.
271
Vln.

274
Vla.
274
Picc.
Fl.
274
Vln.
277
Vla.
277
Picc.
Fl.
277
Vln.

282
Vla.
282
Picc.
Fl.
282
Vln.
285
Vla.
285
Picc.
Fl.
285
Vln.

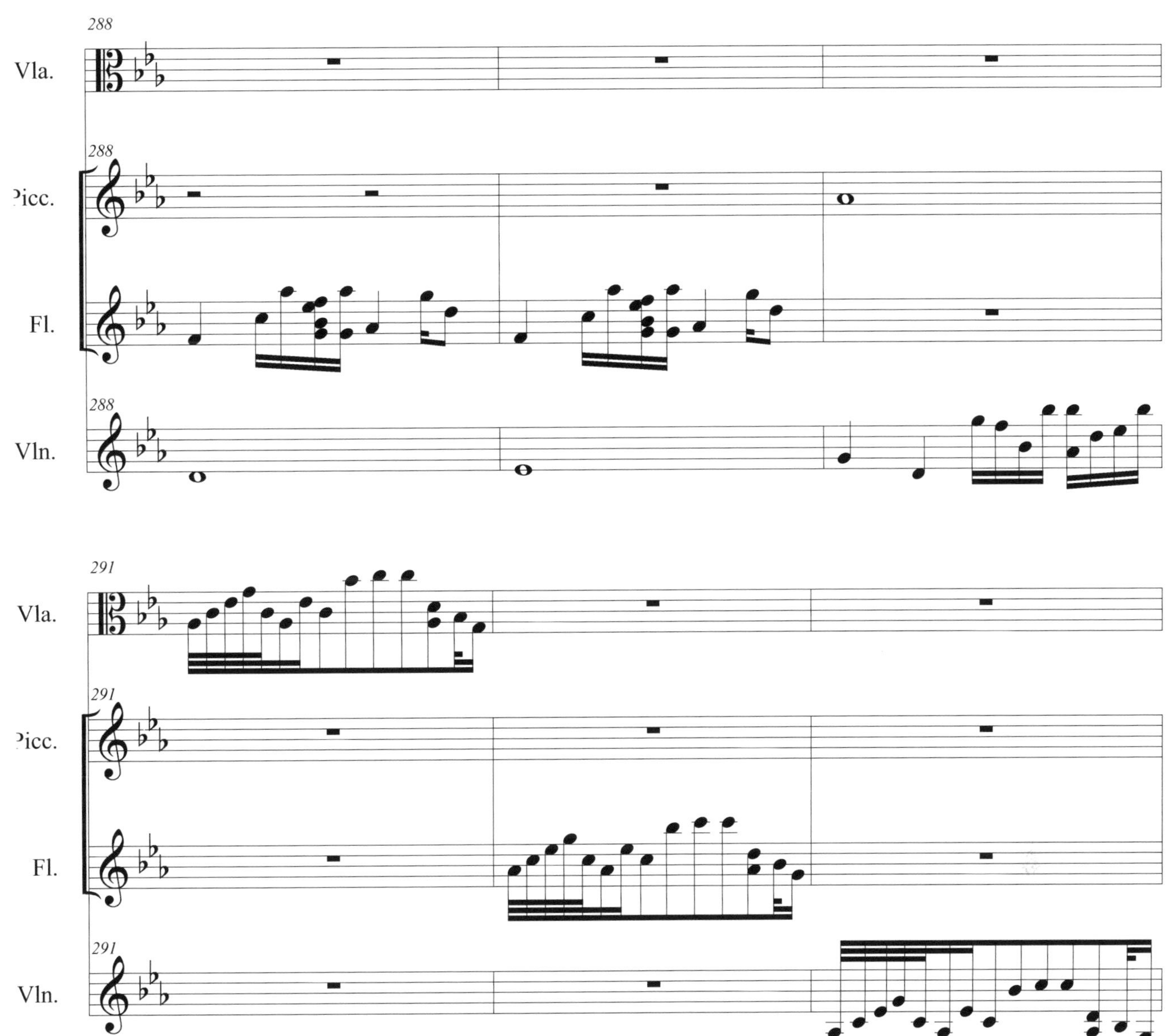
288
Vla.
288
Picc.
Fl.
288
Vln.
291
Vla.
291
Picc.
Fl.
291
Vln.

294
Vla.
294
Picc.
Fl.
294
Vln.
297
Vla.
297
Picc.
Fl.
297
Vln.

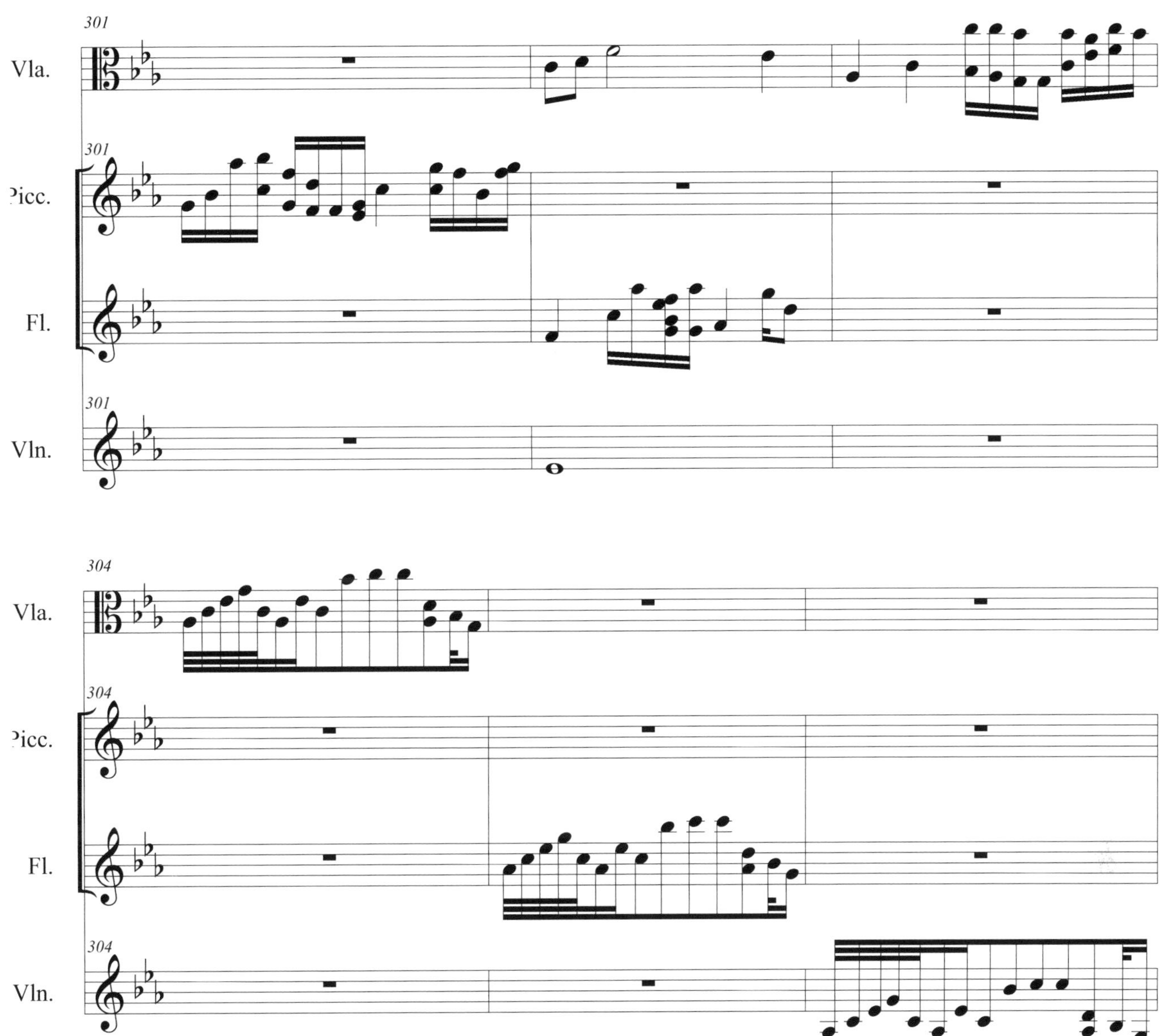
301
Vla.
301
Picc.
Fl.
301
Vln.
304
Vla.
304
Picc.
Fl.
304
Vln.

307
Vla.
307
Picc.
Fl.
307
Vln.
310
Vla.
310
Picc.
Fl.
310
Vln.

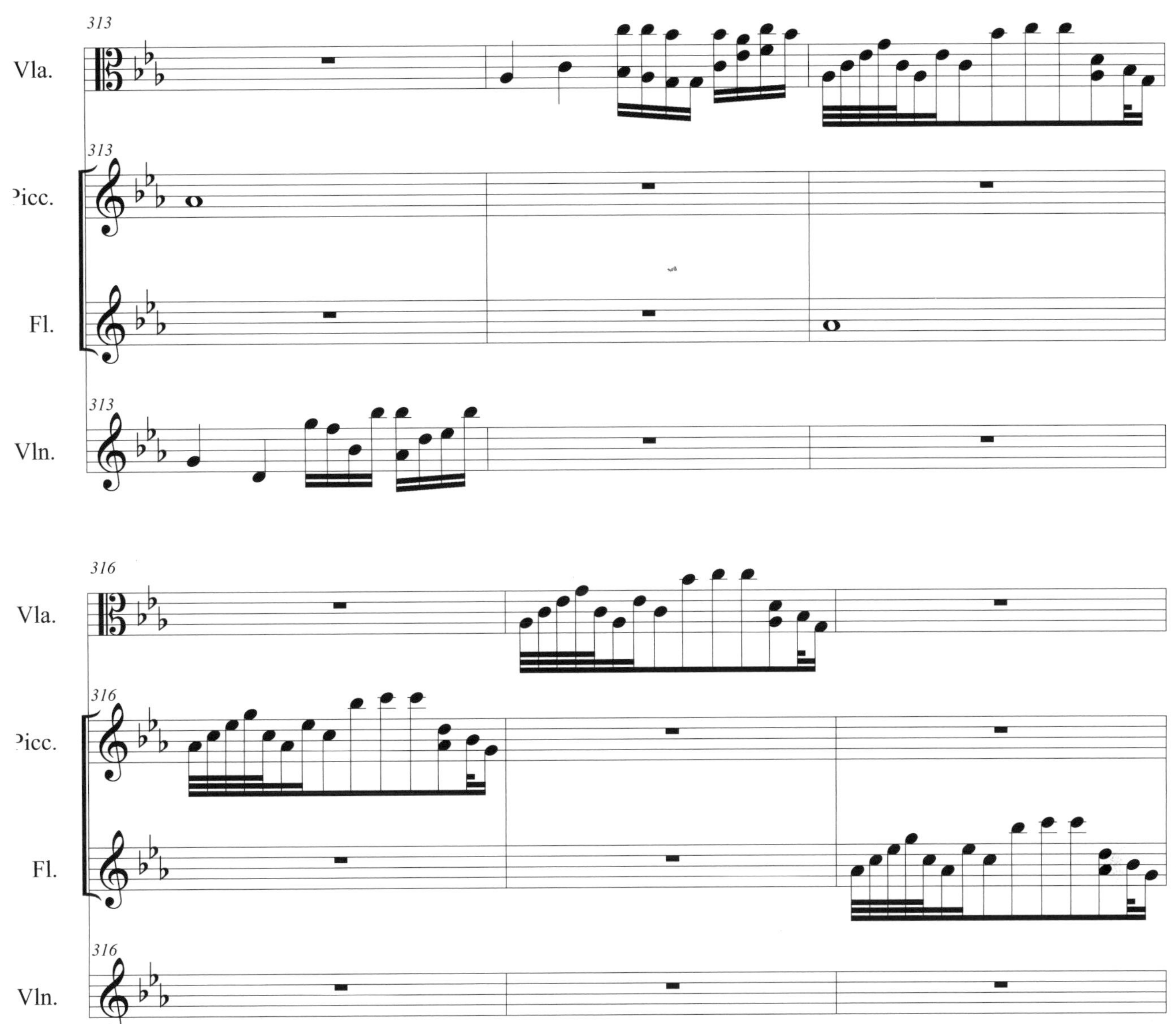
313
Vla.
313
Picc.
Fl.
313
Vln.
316
Vla.
316
Picc.
Fl.
316
Vln.

319
Vla.
319
Picc.
Fl.
319
Vln.
322
Vla.
322
Picc.
Fl.
322
Vln.

325
Vla.
325
Picc.
Fl.
325
Vln.
331
Vla.
331
Picc.
Fl.
331
Vln.

336
Vla.
336
Picc.
Fl.
336
Vln.
341
Vla.
341
Picc.
Fl.
341
Vln.

Symphony No 2, Op 36, in C Minor

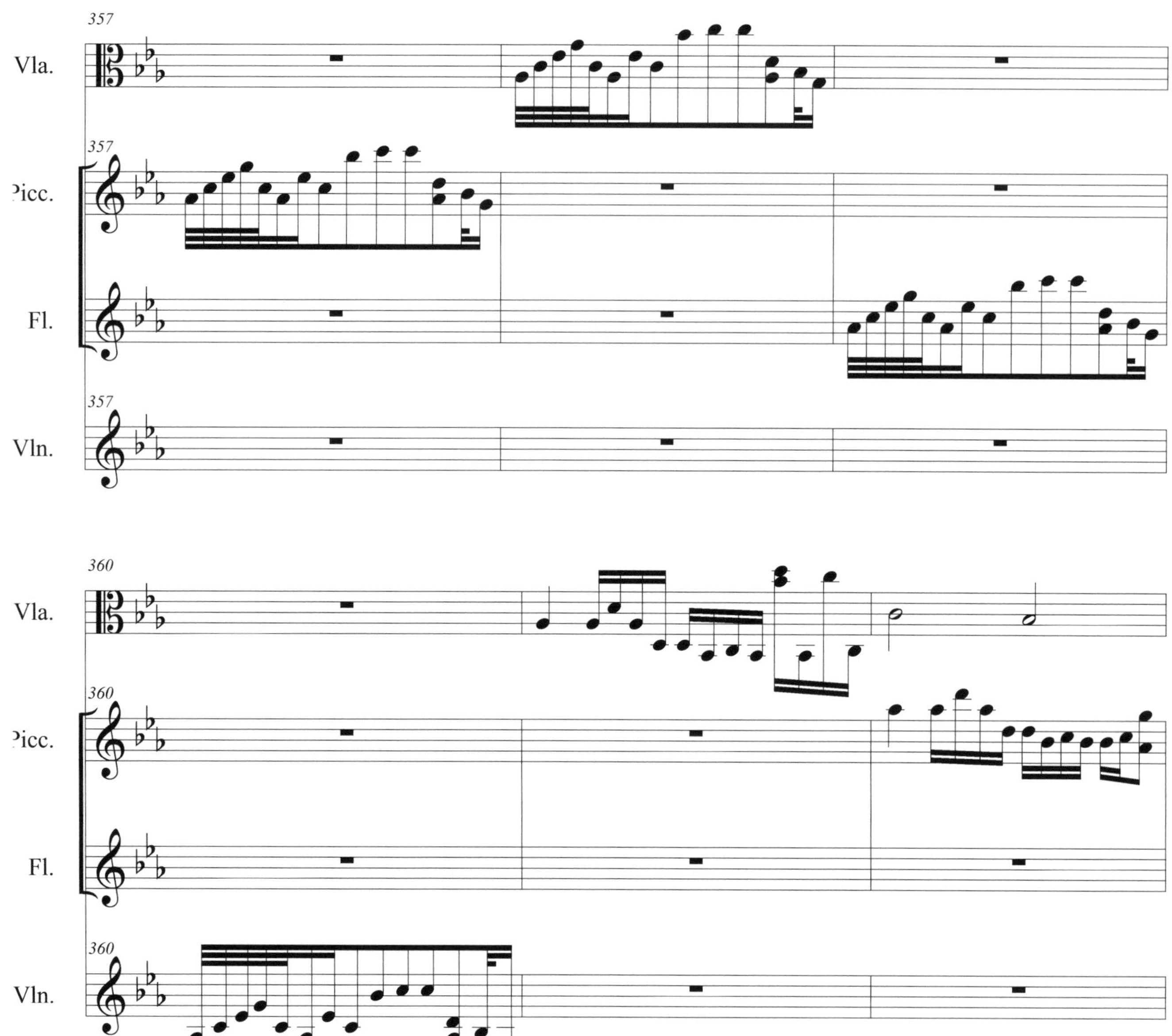
357
Vla.
357
Picc.
Fl.
357
Vln.
360
Vla.
360
Picc.
Fl.
360
Vln.

363
Vla.
363
Picc.
Fl.
363
Vln.
366
Vla.
366
Picc.
Fl.
366
Vln.

369
Vla.
369
Picc.
Fl.
369
Vln.
373
Vla.
373
Picc.
Fl.
373
Vln.

My Carrier Pigeon is inspired by my real Carrier Pigeon. When I was teenager I used to trade pigeons and kept many expensive pigeons as a hobby. Several years before I leave Egypt for America I sold all my expensive pigeons and I was only making wooden nests and cages for the parakeets which I had 200 hundreds couples of them. I also sold the parakeets to get ready for America.

After I sold all pigeons, one Carrier Pigeon returned to me. I thought I have no place for him in my apartment and I sold this particular Carrier Pigeon several time and he returned to me. I sold him in another city and he also returned to me.

I decided to keep him inside the apartment. In my bedroom he used to sleep with me. During the day he flies in the apartment and lands on the furniture. I open the balcony's door for him to fly around the building where I used to live. He spends his day on the balcony's fence. In the evening he goes inside and ends in my bedroom during the night.

For several years before I came to America this pigeon and my two dogs, Liaka and Tosca lived with me. A few months before I came to America, all of the sudden, the dogs and the pigeon died natural deaths.

Score

My Carrier Pigeon

Dr. Anis I. Milad

My Carrier Pigeon

My Carrier Pigeon

Score

It Would Be Scary If I Knew

Dr. Anis I. Milad

It Would Be Scary If I Knew

It Would Be Scary If I Knew

It Would Be Scary If I Knew

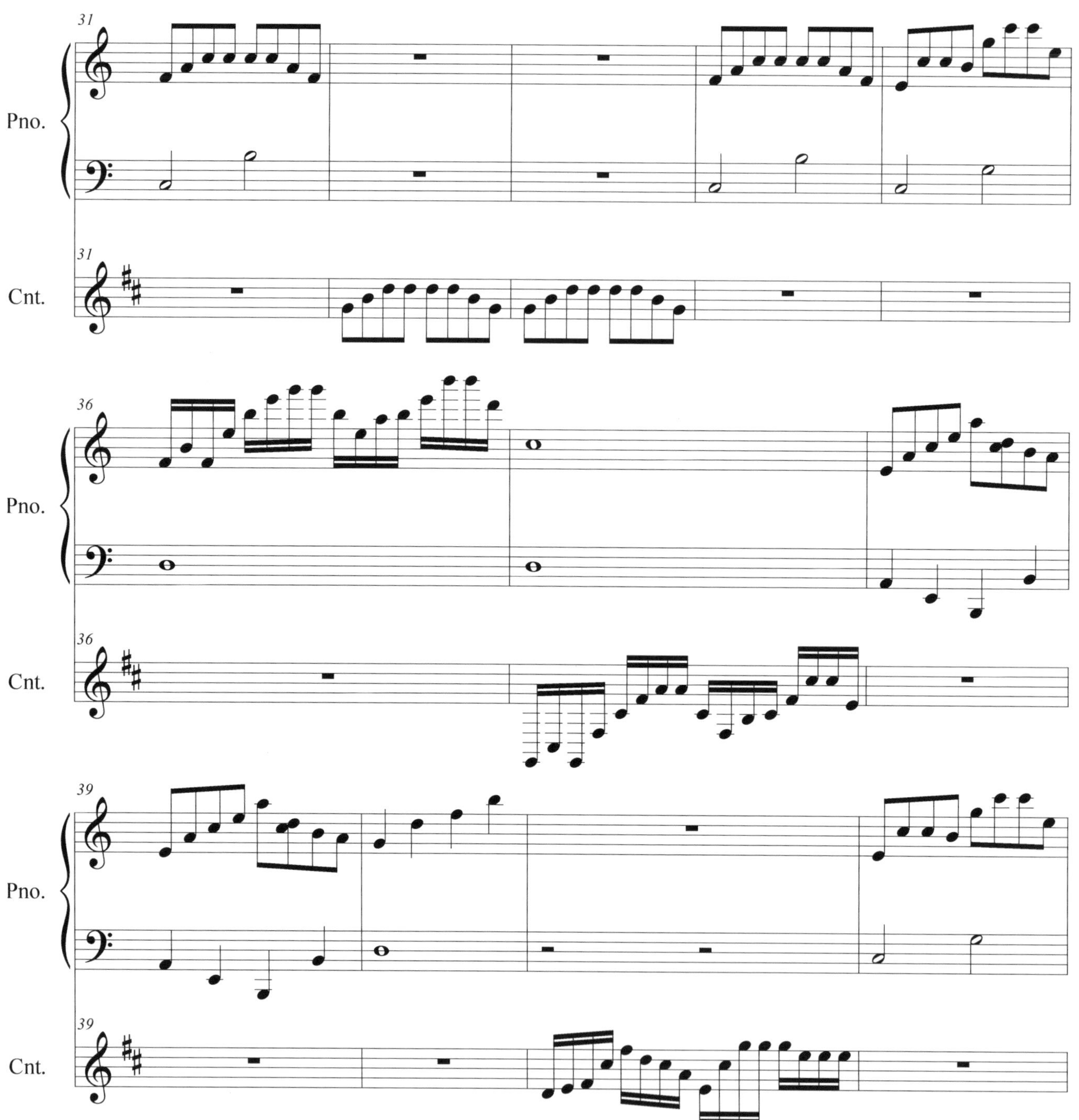

It Would Be Scary If I Knew

It Would Be Scary If I Knew

It Would Be Scary If I Knew

It Would Be Scary If I Knew

It Would Be Scary If I Knew

It Would Be Scary If I Knew

It Would Be Scary If I Knew

It Would Be Scary If I Knew

It Would Be Scary If I Knew

133
Pno.
133
Cnt.
136
Pno.
136
Cnt.
139
Pno.
139
Cnt.

Score

Lauren, My Daughter Vickie, Salwa, Nadia, and Nadia

Dr. Anis I. Milad

16
:Alt.
16
.Gtr.
16
imp.
21
:Alt.
21
.Gtr.
21
imp.
26
:Alt.
26
.Gtr.
26
imp.

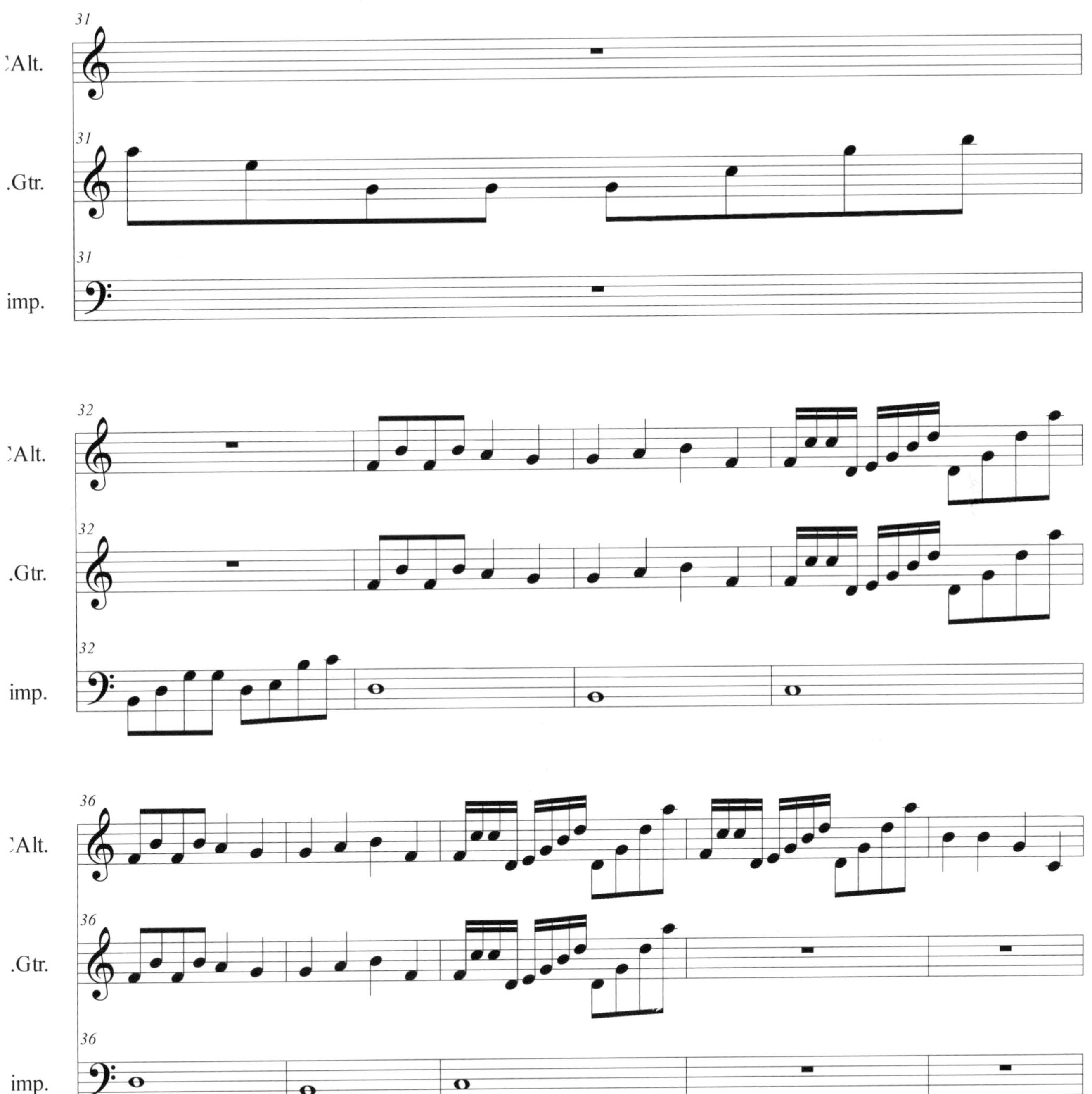
31
:Alt.
31
.Gtr.
31
imp.
32
:Alt.
32
.Gtr.
32
imp.
36
:Alt.
36
.Gtr.
36
imp.

41
:Alt.
.Gtr.
imp.
46
51

56
:Alt.
.Gtr.
imp.
61
66

71
:Alt.
71
.Gtr.
71
imp.
76
:Alt.
76
.Gtr.
76
imp.
81
:Alt.
81
.Gtr.
81
imp.

86
:Alt.
86
.Gtr.
86
imp.
91
:Alt.
91
.Gtr.
91
imp.
96
:Alt.
96
.Gtr.
96
imp.

101
:Alt.
.Gtr.
imp.
106
111

116
:Alt.
.Gtr.
imp.
121
126

131
:Alt.
131
.Gtr.
131
imp.
136
:Alt.
136
.Gtr.
136
imp.
141
:Alt.
141
.Gtr.
141
imp.

Score

Mighty Dreamer

Dr. Anis I. Milad

Mighty Dreamer

Mighty Dreamer

27
Pno.
Cnt.
.Gtr.
29
Pno.
Cnt.
.Gtr.

Mighty Dreamer

Mighty Dreamer

Mighty Dreamer

Mighty Dreamer

Mighty Dreamer

Mighty Dreamer

79
Pno.
Cnt.
.Gtr.
84
Pno.
Cnt.
.Gtr.

Mighty Dreamer

96
Pno.
Cnt.
.Gtr.
98
Pno.
Cnt.
.Gtr.

100
Pno.
100
Cnt.
100
.Gtr.
104
Pno.
104
Cnt.
104
.Gtr.

109
Pno.
109
Cnt.
109
.Gtr.
114
Pno.
114
Cnt.
114
.Gtr.

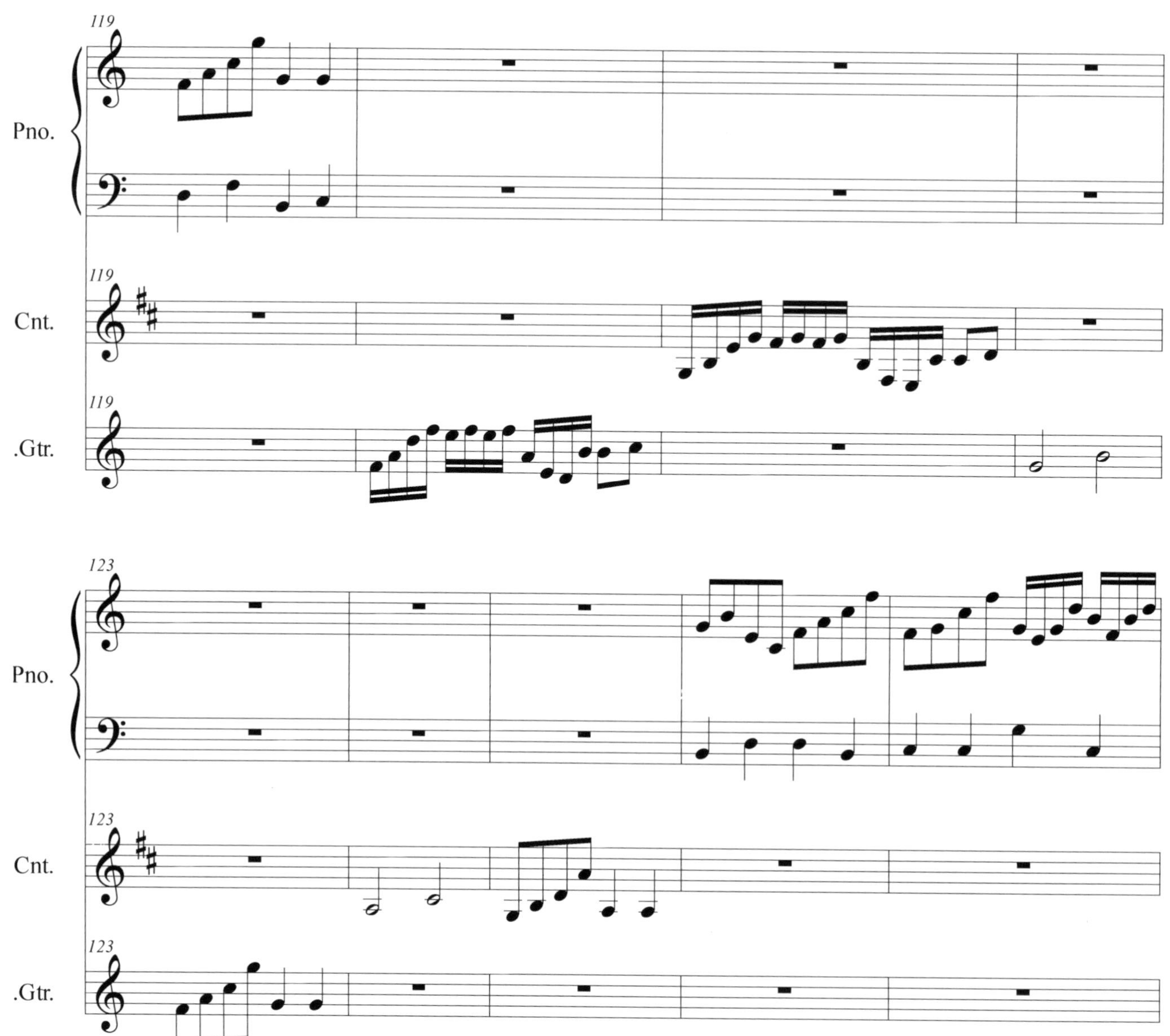
119
Pno.
119
Cnt.
119
.Gtr.
123
Pno.
123
Cnt.
123
.Gtr.

Mighty Dreamer

133
Pno.
Cnt.
.Gtr.
135
Pno.
Cnt.
.Gtr.

Mighty Dreamer

Score

Waiting

Dr. Anis I. Milad

Waiting

Waiting

Waiting

Waiting

Waiting

Waiting

Waiting

91
Pno.
.Gtr.
T
96
Pno.
.Gtr.
T

Waiting

Waiting

126
Pno.
126
.Gtr.
126
T
132
Pno.
132
.Gtr.
132
T

137
Pno.
137
.Gtr.
137
T
142
Pno.
142
.Gtr.
142
T

Waiting

160
Pno.
.Gtr.
T
166
Pno.
.Gtr.
T

171
Pno.
171
.Gtr.
171
T
177
Pno.
177
.Gtr.
177
T

Waiting